Making Sense of Statistics

Statistics

A Conceptual Overview

Fourth Edition

Fred Pyrczak
California State University, Los Angeles

Pyrczak Publishing
P.O. Box 250430 ❖ Glendale, CA 91225

"Pyrczak Publishing" is an imprint of Fred Pyrczak, Publisher, A California Corporation.

Although the author and publisher have made every effort to ensure the accuracy and completeness of information contained in this book, we assume no responsibility for errors, inaccuracies, omissions, or any inconsistency herein. Any slights of people, places, or organizations are unintentional.

Project Director: Monica Lopez.

Editorial assistance provided by Cheryl Alcorn, Randall R. Bruce, Karen M. Disner, Brenda Koplin, Jack Petit, Erica Simmons, and Sharon Young.

Cover design by Robert Kibler and Larry Nichols.

Printed in the United States of America by Malloy, Inc.

ISBN 1-884585-70-1

Contents

Continued →

Introduction

Four types of students need a conceptual overview of statistics.

1. Students who are preparing to be consumers of empirical research and need basic concepts in order to interpret the statistics reported by others in journals, at conferences, and in reports prepared by their supervisors and coworkers.

2. Students who are taking a traditional introductory statistics course and are getting lost in the details of deriving formulas, computing statistics, and sorting through an overload of theory. For them, this book is an ideal supplement.

3. Students who are taking an introductory statistics course in which computers are used for all major calculations but need a text that helps them understand the meaning of their output. For them, this book may be used as the main textbook.

4. Students who have taken a statistics course but need to review essential concepts in preparation for a subsequent course for which statistics is a prerequisite or in preparation for planning their theses and dissertations.

Coverage

The coverage is highly selective. To be included in this book, a statistical technique had to be one that is almost universally included in introductory statistics courses and is widely reported in journals. Once students understand and feel comfortable with the statistics that meet these criteria, they should find it easy to master additional statistical concepts.

Computations and Formulas

You will find no formulas and very few computational procedures described in the body of this book. I have assumed that for some students a noncomputational approach is best for developing an understanding of the meaning of statistics. For students who are becoming consumers of research, this may be all that is needed. For others, computers can handle the computations; such students need to know which statistics are available for various purposes and how to interpret them.

Steps in Using This Book

To get the most from this book, I suggest that you follow these steps: (1) read a section while ignoring all references to footnotes and appendices since these contain information that may distract you as you master essential concepts; (2) read the section again, pausing to read the footnotes and appendices when you encounter references to them; (3) read the summary statements in the sidebars for review; and (4) answer the exercise questions at the end of the section.

If you have not studied statistics, you will find that most of the concepts in this book are entirely new to you. It is not realistic to expect to skim the text once to achieve full mastery. In addition, pilot tests indicate that students who read each section twice before answering the end-of-section questions mastered the concepts more quickly than those who read it only once. The latter did more hunting and pecking through the text to look for answers, which is a slow process that does not provide an overview and leads to errors. Thus, you should save time and achieve greater mastery by following the recommended steps faithfully.

Five multiple-choice items for each section of this book are included near the end of this book in the Comprehensive Review Questions. While these were designed to help students prepare for midterm and comprehensive final exams, they may be used at any time during the course when review is needed.

New to the Fourth Edition

This edition provides greater coverage of correlational statistics with the addition of two new sections: Section 15: Scattergram, and Section 16: Multiple Correlation. There is also more emphasis on sampling as it relates to inferential statistics with a new section on sample size (Section 18). Finally, most of the end-of-chapter exercises contain more exercise items than they did in previous editions. This provides more opportunities for students to practice their newly acquired skills.

Acknowledgments

I am grateful to Dr. Deborah M. Oh, Dr. Robert Morman, and Dr. Patricia Bates Simun, all of California State University, Los Angeles; as well as Dr. Roger A. Stewart, University of Wyoming; Dr. Richard Rasor of American River College; and Dr. Matthew Giblin of Southern Illinois University, Carbondale, for their helpful comments on the various drafts of this book. Errors and omissions remain the responsibility of the author.

Fred Pyrczak
Los Angeles

Part A

The Research Context

Notes:

Section 1

The Empirical Approach
to Knowledge

Empiricism refers to using direct observation to obtain knowledge. Thus, the *empirical approach* to acquiring knowledge is based on making observations of individuals or objects of interest.[1] Note that making *everyday observations* is an application of the empirical approach. For instance, if we observe that a traffic officer regularly hides behind the bushes at a certain intersection and frequently issues tickets at that location, we might say we *know* that someone who runs a stop sign at that intersection is likely to get a ticket. Unfortunately, generalizations based on everyday observations are often misleading. Here is an example:

> Suppose you observe that most of your friends and acquaintances plan to vote in favor of a school bond measure to build new schools. Unless they are a good cross section of the electorate, which is unlikely, you may be wrong if you generalize to the population of voters and predict that the measure will pass in the election.

Most researchers systematically use the empirical approach to acquire knowledge. When they do, we say that they are engaging in *empirical research.* A major distinction between empirical research and everyday observation is that empirical research is planned in advance. Based on a theory or hunch, researchers develop research questions and then plan *whom, how, when*, and *under what circumstances* to observe in order to answer the questions.[2]

1. They plan *whom* (or *what*) to observe. It could be all mentally ill patients in a hospital ward or all public school teachers in Pennsylvania. These are known as *populations*. When a population is large, researchers often plan to observe only a *sample* (i.e., a subset of a population). Planning how to draw an ade-

The empirical *approach* is based on observation.

Everyday observation is an example of the empirical approach.

Generalizations based on everyday observations are often misleading.

Researchers plan *whom, how,* and *when* to observe.

Planning how to draw a *sample* from a *population* is important in conducting valid research.

---

[1] See endnotes at the end of this section.

quate sample is, of course, important in conducting valid research.[3]

2. They plan *how* to observe by deciding whether to construct new measuring instruments or select instruments that have been developed by others. For instance, researchers might review existing multiple-choice tests and select those that are most valid for answering their research questions. They also might build or adopt existing interview schedules, questionnaires, personality scales, etc., to use in making observations.[4]

Measuring instruments are constructed or selected.

3. They plan *when* the observations will be made. For instance, will the observations be made in the morning or late at night? Researchers realize that the timing of their observations may affect the results of their investigations.

Timing and circumstances of the observations may affect the results.

4. They plan to make the observations *under particular circumstances*. For instance, will the observations be made in a quiet room or in a busy shopping mall? Will the observations be made in the presence of a treatment such as an experimental drug?[5]

Unfortunately, not all plans are good, and even the best plans often cannot be fully executed because of physical, ethical, legal, and/or financial constraints. Thus, empirical research varies in quality, and flawed research can be just as misleading as everyday observations often are.

Flawed research can be misleading.

The observations that researchers make result in data. The data might be the names of political candidates for whom participants plan to vote or they might be scores on a scale that measures depression. Large amounts of data need to be organized and summarized, which is a primary function of statistical analysis. For instance, a researcher could summarize the data from an election poll by computing the percentage who plan to vote for each candidate, or a researcher could summarize depression scores by computing an average score. These and many other statistics are described in this book.

Large amounts of data need to be organized and summarized, which is a primary function of statistics.

Notes on Terminology for Referring to Participants in Research

The term *subjects* is the traditional term for referring to the individuals being studied. In recent decades, researchers have increasingly used the term *participants*, which implies that the individuals being studied have freely consented to participate in the research. Note, however, that the term *subjects* is still appropriate when those being studied have not consented to participate. Examples are animals used in medical and psychological research as well as individuals who are observed unobtrusively without their consent, such as adolescents who are observed in a shopping mall without their knowledge.

> The term *participant* is used when individuals have consented.
>
> The term *subject* is appropriate when there is no consent.

In addition to *subjects* and *participants*, other terms that are widely used by researchers are *respondents*, which is most frequently used when individuals respond to a survey such as a political poll, and *examinees*, which is sometimes used when referring to participants who have taken an examination, such as an achievement test, in research on the validity of the test.

Because the term *participants* is, by far, the predominant term used in research reports in the social and behavioral sciences, it is used throughout this book.

> The term *participants* is predominant.

Endnotes

[1] Other approaches are (1) *mathematical deduction*, as when we deduce a proof in mathematics based on certain assumptions and definitions, and (2) *reliance on authority*, such as relying on a dictator's pronouncements as a source of knowledge.

[2] Research questions are the heart of all empirical research. When a researcher predicts the answer to a research question prior to conducting research, we say that he or she has a *hypothesis*. In other words, a *hypothesis* is a prediction of the outcome of research.

[3] Sampling methods are described in Sections 3, 17, and 18.

[4] "Observations" might be direct, such as watching adolescents in a multiracial group interact with each other, *or* they might be indirect, such as having adolescents respond to a questionnaire on how they would interact in an interracial setting.

[5] When researchers administer treatments, the study is classified as an *experiment*. Experiments are discussed in the next section of this book.

Exercise for Section 1

Factual Questions

1. The term *empiricism* refers to what?

2. Does everyday observation employ the empirical approach?

3. When researchers systematically use the empirical approach to acquire knowledge, we say that they are engaging in what?

4. What is the name for a subset of a population?

5. Which type of planning involves constructing or selecting measuring instruments? (Circle one.)
   A. whom   B. how   C. when   D. under what circumstances

6. Even the best plans for research often cannot be fully executed for physical reasons. According to this section of the book, what are some of the other reasons for this?

7. The observations that researchers make result in what?

8. Are the data that researchers collect always "scores"?

9. In recent decades, researchers have increasingly used what term to refer to the individuals being studied?

Questions for Discussion

10. Do you think that the opinions of your friends and acquaintances are good predictors of the outcomes of elections? Why? Why not?

11. Try to recall an instance in which you were misled by an everyday observation. Briefly describe it here.

12. Try to remember an instance in which you read or heard about empirical research that you suspected was flawed. Briefly describe here what you suspected.

Section 2

Types of Empirical Research

A fundamental distinction is whether research is *experimental* or *nonexperimental*. An *experiment* is a study in which treatments are given to see how the participants respond to them. We all conduct informal experiments in our everyday lives. Here are three examples:

- We might try a new laundry detergent (the treatment) to see if our clothes are cleaner (the response) than when we used our old brand.

- A teacher might bring to class a new short story (the treatment) to see if students enjoy it (the response).

- A waiter might try being more friendly (the treatment) to see if it increases his tips (the response).

In an experiment, the treatments are called the *independent variable*, and the responses are called the *dependent variable*. Independent variables are administered so that researchers can observe possible changes in dependent variables.

Clearly, the purpose of experiments is to identify *cause-and-effect relationships*, in which the independent variable is the possible cause and the dependent variable demonstrates the possible effect. When the hypothetical waiter mentioned above tries being friendlier, he is interested in finding out whether the increased friendliness (the independent variable) *causes* increased tips (the dependent variable).

Unfortunately, informal experiments can be misleading. For instance, suppose the waiter notices that when he is friendlier, he gets larger tips than when he is less friendly. Did the increased friendliness *cause* the increase in the tips? The answer is not clear. Perhaps, by chance, the evening that the waiter tried being more friendly, he happened to have customers who were more generous. Perhaps an advice columnist published a column that day on tipping, which urged people to be more generous when tipping waiters and waitresses. Perhaps the waiter was not only more friendly but, unconsciously, also more efficient, and his increased efficiency and not his increased friendliness caused the increase in tips. The possible alter-

An experiment is a study in which treatments are given and responses to them are observed.

Treatments are called the independent variable and responses are called the dependent variable.

The purpose of experiments is to determine cause-and-effect relationships.

Unless it is properly planned, there may be many alternative explanations for the results of an experiment.

native explanations are almost endless unless an experiment is planned in advance to eliminate them.

How could we conduct an experiment on friendliness and tipping that would have a clearer interpretation? The answer is by having an appropriate control condition. For instance, we could have the waiter be friendlier to every alternate party of customers. These customers would constitute the *experimental group.* The remaining customers that receive the normal amount of friendliness would be referred to as the *control group.* In addition, we could monitor the waiter's behavior to be sure it is the same in all respects for both groups of customers except for the degree of friendliness. Then, statistics could be used to compare the average tips earned under the more friendly condition with those earned under the less friendly condition.

An appropriate control condition is an essential characteristic of good experiments.

A *nonexperimental study*, which is sometimes called a *descriptive study*, is defined as a study in which observations are made to determine the status of what exists at a given point in time *without* the administration of treatments. An example is a survey in which a researcher wants to determine participants' attitudes. In such a study, researchers strive *not* to change the participants' attitudes. They do this by avoiding leading questions and having the interviewers remain neutral in tone and mannerisms. If the sample is properly drawn and well-crafted questions are asked, a researcher can obtain solid data on the attitudes held by participants. Note, however, that the researcher who has conducted such a nonexperimental study has not gathered data on how to change attitudes. To do this, he or she would need to conduct an experiment.[1]

A nonexperimental study is one in which no treatments are administered.

Endnote

[1] For some important causal questions, it is not possible to conduct an experiment. For instance, in studying the effects of smoking and health, it would be unethical to encourage or force some human participants to smoke while forbidding others to do so. In such situations, researchers must use data collected in nonexperimental studies to explore causality.

Exercise for Section 2

Factual Questions

1. In which type of study are treatments given in order to see how participants respond?

2. In an experiment, are the responses the "independent variable" *or* the "dependent variable"?

3. What is the purpose of an experiment?

4. In an experiment, a researcher administered various dosage levels of aspirin to different groups of participants in order to determine the effects of the various dosage levels on heart attack rates. In this study, "heart attack rates" is the (circle one)

   A. dependent variable.   B. independent variable.

5. In an experiment, a researcher used group counseling with some participants and used individual counseling with other participants in order to study the effectiveness of the two types of counseling on raising the participants' self-esteem. In this study, the two types of counseling constitute the (circle one)

   A. dependent variable.   B. independent variable.

6. In which type of study do researchers try *not* to change the participants?

7. What is the definition of a *nonexperimental study?*

Questions for Discussion

8. Briefly describe an informal experiment that you recently conducted. Were there alternative explanations for the responses you observed?

9. Do you think that both *nonexperimental* and *experimental* studies have a legitimate role to play in the acquisition of scientific knowledge? Why? Why not?

Notes:

Section 3

Introduction to Sampling

A *population* consists of all members of a group in which a researcher has an interest. It may be small, such as all psychiatrists affiliated with a particular hospital, or it may be large, such as all high school seniors in a state. When populations are large, researchers usually sample. A *sample* is a subset of a population. For instance, we might be interested in the attitudes of all registered nurses in Texas toward people with AIDS. The nurses would constitute the population. If we administered an AIDS attitude scale to all these nurses, we would be studying the population, and the summarized results (such as averages) would be referred to as *parameters*. If we studied only a sample of the nurses, the summarized results would be referred to as *statistics*.

No matter how a sample is drawn, it is always possible that the *statistics* obtained by studying the sample do not accurately reflect the *population parameters* that would have been obtained if the entire population had been studied. In fact, researchers almost always expect some amount of error as a result of sampling.

If sampling creates errors, why do researchers sample? First, for economic and physical reasons it is not always possible to study an entire population. Second, with proper sampling, highly reliable results can be obtained. Furthermore, with proper sampling, the amount of error to allow for in the interpretation of the resulting data can be estimated with inferential statistics, which are covered in Part D of this book.

Freedom from *bias* is the most important characteristic of a good sample. A bias exists whenever some members of a population have a greater chance of being selected for inclusion in a sample than other members of the population. Here are some examples of biased samples:

- A professor wishes to study the attitudes of all sophomores at a college (the population) but asks only those enrolled in her introductory psychology class (the sample) to participate in

A *population* consists of all members of a group.

A *sample* is a subset of a population.

Populations yield *parameters*.

Samples yield *statistics*.

A *bias* is created when some members of a population have a greater chance of being selected than others.

the study. Note that only those in the class have a chance of being selected; other sophomores have no chance.

- An individual wants to predict the results of a citywide election (the population) but asks the intentions of only voters whom he encounters in a large shopping mall (the sample). Note that only those in the mall have a chance of being selected; other voters have no chance.

- A magazine editor wants to determine the opinions of all rifle owners (the population) on a gun-control measure but mails questionnaires only to those who subscribe to her magazine (the sample). Note that only subscribers to her magazine have a chance to respond; other rifle owners have no chance.

In the three examples immediately above, *samples of convenience* (or *accidental samples*) were used, increasing the odds that some members of a population will be selected while reducing the odds that others members will be selected. In addition to the obvious bias in the examples, there is an additional problem. Even those who do have a chance of being included in the samples may refuse to participate. This problem is often referred to as the problem of *volunteerism* (also called *self-selection bias*). Volunteerism is presumed to create an additional source of bias because those who decide not to participate have no chance of being included. Furthermore, many studies comparing participants (i.e., volunteers) with non-participants suggest that participants tend to be more highly educated and tend to come from higher socioeconomic status (SES) groups than their counterparts. Efforts to reduce the effects of volunteerism include offering rewards; stressing to potential participants the importance of the study; and making it easy for individuals to respond, such as providing them with a stamped, self-addressed envelope.

To eliminate bias in the selection of individuals for a study, some type of *random sampling* is needed. A classic type of random sampling is *simple random sampling*. This technique gives each member of a population an equal chance of being selected. A simple way to accomplish this with a small population is to put the names of all members of a population on slips of paper, thoroughly mix the slips, and have a blindfolded assistant select the number desired for the sample.[1] After the names have been selected, efforts must be made to encourage all those selected to participate. If some refuse, as

Samples of convenience are biased.

Volunteerism in sampling is presumed to create a bias.

In *simple random sampling*, each member of a population is given an equal chance of being selected.

12

often happens, a biased sample is obtained even though all members of the population had an equal chance to have their names selected.

Suppose that a researcher is fortunate. He or she selected names using simple random sampling and obtained the cooperation of everyone selected. In this case, the researcher has obtained an *unbiased sample*. Can the researcher be certain that the results obtained from the sample accurately reflect those results that would have been obtained by studying the entire population? Certainly not. The possibility of random errors still exists. Random errors (created by random selection) are called *sampling errors* by statisticians. At random (i.e., by chance), the researcher may have selected a disproportionately large number of Democrats, males, low SES group members, and so on. Such errors make the sample unrepresentative and therefore may lead to incorrect results.

If both biased and unbiased sampling are subject to error, why do researchers prefer unbiased random sampling? They prefer it for two reasons: (1) inferential statistics, which are described in Part D of this book, enable researchers to estimate the amount of error to allow for when analyzing the results from unbiased samples, and (2) the amount of sampling error obtained from unbiased samples tends to be small when large samples are used.

While using large samples helps to limit the amount of random error, it is important to note that selecting a large sample does not correct for errors due to bias. For instance, if the individual who is trying to predict the results of a citywide election in the earlier example is very persistent and spends weeks at the shopping mall asking shoppers how they intend to vote, the individual will obtain a very large sample of people who may differ from the population of voters in various ways, such as being more affluent, having more time to spend shopping, and so on. This illustrates that increasing the size of a biased sample does not reduce the amount of error due to bias.

Despite the above discussion, it is *not* true that all research in which biased samples are used is worthless. There are many situations in which researchers have no choice but to use biased samples. For instance, for ethical and legal reasons, much medical research is conducted using volunteers who are willing to risk taking a new medication or undergoing a new surgical procedure. If promising results are obtained in initial studies, larger studies with better (but usually still biased) samples are undertaken. At some point, despite the

---

Simple random sampling identifies an *unbiased sample*.

Random sampling produces *sampling errors*.

Selecting a large sample does not correct for errors due to bias.

Often, researchers have no choice but to use biased samples.

possible role of bias, decisions such as Food and Drug Administration approval of a new drug need to be made on the basis of data obtained with biased samples. Little progress would be made in most fields if the results of all studies with biased samples were summarily dismissed.

At the same time, it is important to note that the statistical remedies for errors due to biased samples are extremely limited. Because researchers usually do not know the extent to which a particular bias has affected their results (e.g., they do not know how nonrespondents to a questionnaire would have answered the questions), it is generally not possible to adjust statistically for errors created by bias. Thus, when biased samples are used, the results of statistical analyses of the data should be viewed with great caution.

Statistical results based on observations of biased samples should be viewed with great caution.

Various methods of random sampling are described in more detail in Section 17 of this book. Considerations in determining sample size are discussed in Section 18.

Endnote

[1] Another method for selecting a *simple random sample* and other types of random samples are described in Section 17.

Exercise for Section 3

Factual Questions

1. What term is used to refer to all members of a group in which a researcher has an interest?

2. If samples yield "statistics," what do populations yield?

3. What is the most important characteristic of a good sample?

4. If a researcher uses a sample of volunteers from a population, should we presume that the sample is biased?

5. What type of sampling eliminates bias in the selection of participants?

6. Briefly describe how one could select a simple random sample.

7. Does random sampling produce sampling errors?

8. The amount of random sampling error obtained from unbiased samples tends to be small when what is done?

9. Is selecting a large sample an effective way to reduce the effects of bias in sampling?

10. According to this section of the book, is all research in which biased samples are used worthless?

Questions for Discussion

11. Are you convinced that using a rather small, unbiased sample is better than using a very large, biased sample? Why? Why not?

12. Be on the lookout for a news report of a scientific study in which a biased sample was used. If you find one, briefly describe it here.

Notes:

Section 4

Scales of Measurement

Scales of measurement (also known as *levels of measurement*) help researchers determine what type of statistical analysis is appropriate for a given set of data. It is important to master the material in this section of the book because it is referred to in a number of others that follow.

The lowest level of measurement is *nominal* (also known as *categorical*). It is helpful to think of this level as the *naming* level because names (i.e., words) are used instead of numbers. Here are four examples:

The lowest level of measurement is *nominal*, which is the *naming level*.

- Participants name the political parties with which they are affiliated.
- Participants name their gender.
- Participants name the states in which they reside.
- Participants name their religious affiliation.

Notice that the categories participants name in these examples do not put the participants in any particular order. There is no basis on which we could all agree for saying that Republicans are either higher or lower than Democrats. The same is true for gender, state of residence, and religious affiliation.

The next level of measurement is *ordinal*. Ordinal measurement puts participants in rank *order* from high to low, but it does *not* indicate how much higher or lower one participant is in relation to another. To understand this level, consider these examples:

Ordinal measurement puts participants in rank *order*.

- Participants are ranked according to their height; the tallest participant is given a rank of 1, the next tallest is given a rank of 2, and so on.
- Three brands of hand lotion are ranked according to consumers' preferences for them.
- High school students rank order the subjects they are taking in school, giving their favorite subject a rank of 1, their next favorite a rank of 2, and so on.

In the examples above, the measurements indicate the relative standings of participants but do not indicate the amount of difference among participants. For instance, we know that a participant with a rank of one is taller than a participant with a rank of two, but we do not know by how much. The first participant may be only one-quarter of an inch taller or may be two feet taller than the second.

The next two levels, *interval* and *ratio*, tell us by *how much* participants differ. For example:

> The height of each participant is measured to the nearest inch.
>
> The number of times each pigeon presses a button in the first minute after receiving a reward is measured.

Notice that if one participant is 5'6" tall and another is 5'8" tall, we know not only the order of the participants, but we also know by how much the participants differ from each other (i.e., two inches). Both *interval* and *ratio* scales have equal intervals. For instance, the difference between three inches and four inches is the same as the difference between five inches and six inches.

In most statistical analyses, *interval* and *ratio* measurements are analyzed in the same way. However, there is a scientific difference between these two levels. An *interval* scale does not have an absolute zero. For instance, if we measure intelligence, we do not know exactly what constitutes absolutely zero intelligence and thus cannot measure the zero point.[1] In contrast, a *ratio* scale has an absolute zero point on its scale.[2] For instance, we know where the zero point is on a tape measure when we measure height.

If you are having trouble mastering levels of measurement, first memorize this environmentally friendly phrase:

$$\boxed{\textsf{No Oil In Rivers}}$$

The first letters of the words (NOIR) are the first letters in the names of the four levels of measurement in order from lowest to highest. Now read this section again and associate the definitions with each level.

Interval and *ratio* scales measure *how much* participants differ from each other.

Ratio scales have an absolute zero; *interval* scales do not.

Endnotes

[1] Most applied researchers treat the scores from standardized tests (except percentile ranks and grade-equivalent scores) as *interval* scales of measurement.

[2] Thus, the ratio scale is the only one for which it is appropriate to compute ratios. For instance, it is appropriate to make statements such as "John is twice as tall as Sam" (a ratio of 2 to 1) only when using a ratio scale.

Exercise for Section 4

Factual Questions

1. What is the name of the lowest scale of measurement?

2. Which level of measurement should be thought of as the "naming" level?

3. Which scale of measurement puts participants in rank order?

4. Which two scales of measurement indicate the amount by which participants differ from each other?

5. Which scale of measurement has an absolute zero?

6. If you measure the weight of participants in pounds, which scale of measurement are you using?

7. If you rank employees from most cooperative to least cooperative, which scale of measurement are you using?

8. If you ask participants to name the country they were born in, which scale of measurement are you using?

9. What phrase should you memorize in order to remember the scales of measurement in order?

10. Which scale of measurement is between the ordinal and ratio scales?

Notes:

Section 5

Descriptive, Correlational, and Inferential Statistics

Descriptive statistics summarize data. For instance, suppose you have the scores on a standardized test for 500 participants. One way to summarize the data is to calculate an *average* score, which indicates how the typical individual scored. You might also determine the *range* of scores from the highest to the lowest score, which would indicate how much the scores vary. These and other descriptive statistics are described in detail in Part B of this book.

Correlational statistics are a special subgroup of descriptive statistics, which are described separately in Part C of this book. The purpose of correlational statistics is to describe the relationship between two or more variables for one group of participants. For instance, suppose a researcher is interested in the predictive validity of a college admissions test. The researcher could collect the admissions scores and the freshman GPAs for a group of college students. To determine the validity of the test for predicting GPAs, a statistic known as a *correlation coefficient* could be computed. Correlation coefficients range in value from 0.00 (no correlation between variables) to 1.00 (a perfect correlation).[1] The meanings of these values are described in detail in Part C.

Inferential statistics are tools that tell us how much confidence we can have when generalizing from a sample to a population.[2] Consider national opinion polls in which carefully drawn samples of only about 1,500 adults are used to estimate the opinions of the entire adult population of the United States. The pollster first calculates *descriptive statistics*, such as the *percentage* of respondents who are in favor of capital punishment and the percentage who are opposed.

Having sampled, a researcher knows that the results may not be accurate because the sample may not be representative. In fact, the pollster knows that there is a high probability that the results are off by at least a small amount. This is why pollsters often mention a *margin of error*, which is an inferential statistic. It is reported as a

Descriptive statistics summarize data.

An *average* is a descriptive statistic.

Inferential statistics are tools that help us generalize from a sample to a population.

A *percentage* is a descriptive statistic.

A *margin of error* is an inferential statistic.

21

warning to readers of research that random sampling may have produced errors, which should be considered when interpreting results. For instance, a weekly news magazine recently reported that 52% of the respondents in a national poll believed that the economy was improving. A footnote in the report indicated that the margin of error was ±2.3. This means that the pollster was confident that the true percentage for the whole population was within 2.3 percentage points of 52% (i.e., 49.7% to 54.3%).

You may recall from Section 3 of this book that a *population* is any group in which a researcher is interested. It may be large, such as all adults age 18 and over who reside in the United States, or it might be small, such as all registered nurses employed by a specific hospital. A study in which all members of a population are included is called a *census*. A census is often feasible and desirable when studying small populations (e.g., an algebra teacher may choose to pretest all students at the beginning of a course). When a population is large, it is more economical to study only a sample of the population. With modern sampling techniques, highly accurate information can be obtained using relatively small samples. Sample size is discussed in detail in Section 18.

> A *census* is a study in which all members of a population are included.

Inferential statistics are *not* needed when analyzing the results of a census because there is no sampling error. The use of inferential statistics for evaluating results when sampling has been used is discussed in Part D of this book.

> *Inferential statistics* are *not* needed when analyzing the results of a census.

Endnotes

[1] Correlation coefficients can also be negative. Negative coefficients are also described in Part C of this book.

[2] The word *inferential* comes from *infer*. When we generalize from a sample to a population, we are *inferring* that the sample is representative of the population.

Exercise for Section 5

Factual Questions

1. Is an *average* a "descriptive statistic" *or* an "inferential statistic"?

2. Is the *range* of a set of scores a "descriptive statistic" *or* an "inferential statistic"?

3. What is the purpose of correlational statistics?

4. If there is no relationship between two sets of scores, what is the value of the correlation coefficient?

5. Inferential statistics are tools that tell us what?

6. Is a margin of error a "descriptive statistic" *or* an "inferential statistic"?

7. A margin of error is reported as a warning to readers that what might have happened?

8. What is the name of the type of study in which all members of a population are included?

9. Why are inferential statistics *not* needed when analyzing the results of a census?

Notes:

Part B

Descriptive Statistics

Notes:

Section 6

Frequencies, Percentages, and Proportions

A *frequency* is the number of participants or cases. Its symbol is *f*.[1] *N*, meaning *number of participants*, is also used to stand for frequency.[2] Thus, if you see in a report that *f* = 23 for a score of 99, you know that 23 participants had a score of 99. Likewise, if you see that *N* = 23 for a score of 99, you know that 23 participants had a score of 99.

A *percentage*, whose symbol is %, indicates the number per hundred who have a certain characteristic. Thus, if you are told that 44% of the registered voters in a town are registered as Democrats, you know that for each 100 registered voters, 44 are Democrats. To determine how many (the *frequency*) are Democrats, multiply the total number of registered voters by .44. Thus, if there are 2,200 registered voters, .44 × 2,200 = 968 are Democrats.

To calculate a percentage, use division. Consider this example: If 22 of 84 gifted children in a sample report being afraid of the dark, determine the percentage by dividing the number who are afraid by the total number of children and then multiply by 100. Thus, 22 ÷ 84 = .2619 × 100 = 26.19%. This result indicates that based on the sample, if you questioned *100 participants* from the same population, you would expect about 26 of them to report being afraid of the dark.

A *proportion* is part of one (1). In the previous paragraph, the proportion of children afraid of the dark is .2619 or .26, which is the answer obtained before multiplying by 100. This means that *twenty-six hundredths* of each child is afraid of the dark. As you can see, proportions are harder to interpret than percentages. Thus, percentages are usually preferred to proportions in all types of reporting. However, do not be surprised if you occasionally encounter proportions in research reports.

When reporting percentages, it is a good idea to also report the underlying frequencies because percentages alone can sometimes be misleading or not provide sufficient information. For instance, if you read that 8% of the foreign-language students at a university were majoring in Russian, you would not have enough information to make informed decisions on how to staff the foreign-language department and how many classes in Russian to offer. If you read that $f = 12$ (8%), based on a total of 150 foreign-language students, you would know that 12 students need to be accommodated.

Percentages are especially helpful when comparing two or more groups of different sizes. Consider these statistics:

	College A	College B
Total number of foreign-language students	$N = 150$	$N = 350$
Russian majors	$N = 12$ (8%)	$N = 14$ (4%)

Notice that the frequencies (indicated by N) tell us that College B has more Russian majors, but the percentages tell us that College A (with 8%) has more Russian majors *per 100* than College B (with only 4%). Clearly, frequencies and percentages convey different types of information.

Endnotes

[1] Note that f is italicized. If you do not have the ability to type in italics, underline the symbol. This applies to almost all statistical symbols. Also, pay attention to the case. A lowercase f stands for *frequency*; an uppercase F stands for another statistic described in Section 24 of this book.

[2] An uppercase N should be used when describing a population; a lowercase n should be used when describing a sample.

Exercise for Section 6

Factual Questions

1. What does *frequency* mean?

2. What is the symbol for *frequency*?

3. For what does N stand?

4. If 21% of kindergarten children are afraid of monsters, how many out of each 100 are afraid?

5. Suppose you read that 20% of a population of 1,000 was opposed to a city council resolution. How many are opposed?

6. What statistic is a part of 1?

7. According to this section, are "percentages" *or* "proportions" easier to interpret?

8. Why is it a good idea to report the underlying frequencies when reporting percentages?

Notes:

Section 7

Shapes of Distributions

The shape of a distribution of a set of scores can be seen by examining a *frequency distribution*, which is a table that shows how many participants have each score. Consider the frequency distribution in Table 7.1. The frequency (i.e., f, which is the number of participants) associated with each score (X) is shown. Examination indicates that most of the participants are near the middle of the distribution (i.e., near a score of 19) and that the participants are spread out on both sides of the middle with the frequencies tapering off.

Table 7.1
Distribution of Depression Scores

X	f
22	1
21	3
20	4
19	8
18	5
17	2
16	0
15	1
	$N = 24$

The shape of a distribution is even clearer when examining a *frequency polygon*, which is a figure (i.e., a drawing) that shows how many participants have each score. The same data shown in Table 7.1 above are shown in the frequency polygon in Figure 7.1 on the next page. For instance, the frequency distribution shows that 3 participants had a score of 21; this same information is displayed in the frequency polygon. The high point in the polygon shows where most of the participants are clustered (in this case, near a score of 19). The tapering off around 19 illustrates how spread out the participants are around the middle.

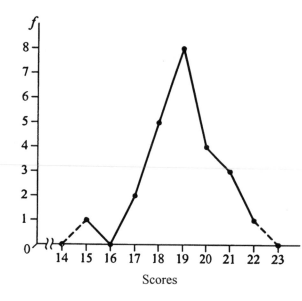

Figure 7.1. Frequency polygon for data in Table 7.1.

When there are many participants, the shape of a polygon becomes smoother and is referred to as a *curve*. The most important shape is that of the *normal curve*, which is often called the *bell-shaped curve*. This curve is illustrated in Figure 7.2 on the next page. The normal curve is important for two reasons. First, it is a shape very often found in nature. For instance, the heights of women in large populations are normally distributed. There are small numbers of very short women, which is why the curve is low on the left; many women are of about average height, which is why the curve is high in the middle; and there are small numbers of very tall women. Here is another example: The average annual rainfall in Los Angeles over the past 110 years has been approximately normal. There have been a very small number of years in which there was extremely little rainfall, many years with about average rainfall, and a very small number of years with a great deal of rainfall. Another reason the normal curve is important is that it is used as the basis for a number of inferential statistics, which are covered in detail in Part D of this book.

The *normal curve* is the most important curve.

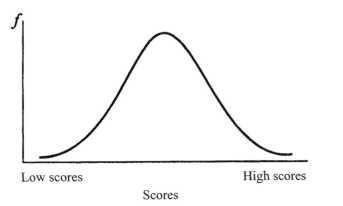

Figure 7.2. A normal distribution.

Some distributions are *skewed*. For instance, if you plot the distribution of income for a large population, in all likelihood you will find that it has a *positive skew* (i.e., is skewed to the right). Examine Figure 7.3 below. It indicates that there are large numbers of people with relatively low incomes; thus, the curve is high on the left. The curve drops off dramatically to the right, forming a long tail pointing to the right. This long tail is created by the small numbers of individuals with very high incomes. Skewed distributions are named for their long tails. On a number line, positive numbers are to the right; hence, the term *positive skew* is used to describe a skewed distribution in which there is a long tail pointing to the right (but no long tail pointing to the left).

A distribution with a *positive skew* has a tail to the right.

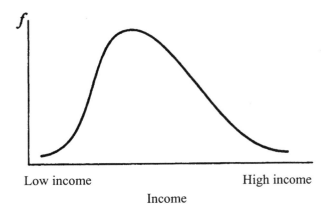

Figure 7.3. A distribution skewed to the right (positive skew).

When the long tail is pointing to the left, a distribution is said to have a *negative skew* (i.e., skewed to the left). See Figure 7.4 below. A negative skew would be found if a large population of individuals was tested on skills in which they have been thoroughly trained. For instance, if a researcher tested a very large population of recent nursing school graduates on very basic nursing skills, a distribution with a negative skew should emerge. There should be large numbers of graduates with high scores, but there should be a long tail pointing to the left, showing that a small number of nurses who, for one reason or another, such as being physically ill on the day the test was administered, did not perform well on the test.

A distribution with a *negative skew* has a tail to the left.

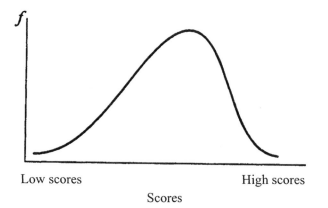

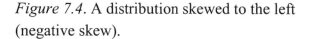

Figure 7.4. A distribution skewed to the left (negative skew).

Bimodal distributions have two high points. A curve such as that in Figure 7.5 is called bimodal even though the two high points are not exactly equal in height. Such a curve is most likely to emerge when human intervention or a rare event has changed the composition of a population. For instance, if a civil war in a country cost the lives of many young adults, the distribution of age after the war might be bimodal, with a dip in the middle. Bimodal distributions are much less frequently found in research than the other types of curves discussed earlier in this section.

A *bimodal distribution* has two high points.

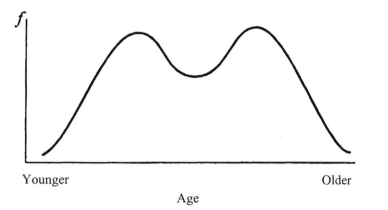

Figure 7.5. A bimodal distribution.

The shape of a distribution has important implications for determining which average to compute—a topic that is discussed in the next two sections of this book.

The shape of a distribution has implications for determining which average to compute.

Exercise for Section 7

Factual Questions

1. What is the name of a table that shows how many participants have each score?

2. What does a frequency polygon show?

3. What is the most important type of curve?

4. Which type of distribution is often found in nature?

5. In a distribution with a negative skew, is the long tail pointing to the "left" *or* to the "right"?

6. When plotted, income in large populations usually has what type of skew?

7. Suppose that on a 100-item multiple-choice test almost all students scored between 95 and 100 but a small scattering of participants scored as low as 20. When plotted as a curve, the distribution will show what type of skew?

8. Suppose that a broad cross section of high school students took a very difficult scholarship examination and almost all scored very low but a very small number scored very high. When plotted as a curve, the distribution will show what type of skew?

9. What is the name of the type of distribution that has two high points?

10. Which type of distribution is much less frequently found in research than the others?

Section 8

The Mean: An Average

The *mean* is the most frequently used average. It is so widely used that it is sometimes simply called the *average*. However, the term "average" is ambiguous because several different types of averages are used in statistics. In this section, the *mean* will be considered. Two other averages will be considered in the next section.

Computation of the mean is easy: sum (i.e., add up) the scores and divide by the number of scores. Here is an example:

The *mean* is the most frequently used average.

Scores: 5, 6, 7, 10, 12, 15
Sum of scores: 55
Number of scores: 6
Computation of mean: 55/6 = 9.166 = 9.17

To compute the *mean*, sum the scores and divide by the number of scores.

Notice in the example above that the answer was computed to three decimal places and rounded to two. In research reports, the mean is usually reported to two decimal places.

There are several symbols for the mean. In academic journals, the most commonly used symbols for the mean are *M* and *m*.[1] In addition, some mathematical statisticians use this symbol:

$$\overline{X}$$

This symbol is pronounced "*X-bar.*" While it is used in some statistics textbooks, it is rarely used in research reports in the social and behavioral sciences.

M and *m* are the most commonly used symbols for the *mean* in academic journals.

The *mean* is defined as "the balance point in a distribution of scores." Specifically, it is *the point around which all the deviations sum to zero.* The example in Table 8.1 on the next page illustrates this characteristic of the mean. The sum of the scores is 60; dividing this by the number of scores (5) yields a mean of 12.00. By subtracting the mean from each score, the *deviations* from the mean are obtained. For instance, the first score in Table 8.1 on the next page is 7. The score (7) minus the mean (12) yields a deviation of –5. Thus, for a score of 7, the deviation is –5.

The *mean* is the balance point in a distribution of scores.

The deviations in the last column of Table 8.1 below sum to zero.[2] (Notice that the negatives cancel out the positives when summing, yielding zero.)

The deviations from the *mean* sum to zero.

Table 8.1
Scores and Their Deviations from Their Mean

Score	Mean	Deviation
7	12.00	−5
11	12.00	−1
11	12.00	−1
14	12.00	2
17	12.00	5
	Sum of deviations = 0	

Note that if you substitute any other number for the mean and perform the calculations in Table 8.1 above, you will *not* get a sum of zero. Only the mean will produce this sum. Thus, saying "the mean equals 12.0" is a shorthand way of saying "the value around which the deviations sum to zero is 12.0."

A major drawback of the mean is that it is drawn in the direction of extreme scores. This is a problem if there are *either* some extremely high scores that pull the mean up *or* some extremely low scores that pull it down. The following is an example of the contributions given to charity by two groups of children expressed in cents:

The *mean* is pulled in the direction of extreme scores, which can be misleading.

Group A: 1, 1, 2, 3, 3, 4, 4, 4, 5, 5, 5, 5, 6, 6, 6, 7, 8, 10, 10, 10, 11
Mean for Group A = 5.52

Group B: 1, 2, 2, 3, 3, 3, 4, 4, 5, 5, 5, 6, 6, 6, 6, 6, 9, 10, 10, 150, 200
Mean for Group B = 21.24

Notice that overall the two distributions are quite similar. Yet the mean for Group B is much higher than the mean for Group A because just two students in Group B gave extremely high contributions of 150 cents and 200 cents. If only the means for the two groups were reported without reporting all the individual contributions, it would suggest that the average student in Group B gave about 21 cents when in fact none of the students made a contribution of about this amount. A distribution that has some extreme scores at one end but not the other is called a *skewed distribution* (see Section 7 to review the meaning of a skewed distribution). The mean is almost always inappropriate for describing the average of a highly skewed distribution. An average that provides a more accurate indication of the score of the typical participant in a skewed distribution is described in the next section of this book.

> The *mean* is inappropriate for describing a highly skewed distribution.

Another limitation of the mean is that it is appropriate only for use with *interval* and *ratio* scales of measurement (see Section 4 to review scales of measurement). Averages that are appropriate for use with data at the nominal and ordinal levels are described in the next section of this book.

> The *mean* should be used only with *interval* and *ratio* scales of measurement.

Note that a synonym for *average* is *measure of central tendency*. Although the latter term is seldom used in research reports in academic journals, you may encounter the term in some statistics texts.

> A synonym for *average* is *measure of central tendency*.

Endnotes

[1] The uppercase *M* should be used for the mean of an entire population, and the lowercase *m* should be used for the mean of a sample drawn from a population.

[2] Note that if the mean is not a whole number, the sum of the deviations may vary slightly from zero due to rounding when determining the mean because a rounded mean is not *precisely* accurate.

Exercise for Section 8

Factual Questions

1. How is the mean computed?

2. What are the most commonly used symbols for the mean in academic journals?

3. For a given distribution, if you subtract the mean from each score to get deviations and then sum the deviations, what will the sum of the deviations equal?

4. Refer to the example in this section of contributions given to charity. Explain why the mean for Group B is much higher than the mean for Group A.

5. If most participants have similar scores but there are a few very high scores, what effect will the very high scores have on the mean?

6. Is the mean usually appropriate for describing the average of a highly skewed distribution?

7. For which scales of measurement is the mean appropriate?

8. The term *measure of central tendency* is synonymous with what other term?

Section 9

Mean, Median, and Mode

The *mean,* which was described in the previous section of this book, is the *balance point* in a distribution. It is the most frequently used average.[1]

The *mean* is the *balance point* in a distribution.

An alternative average is the *median.* It is the value in a distribution that has 50% of the cases above it and 50% of the cases below it. Thus, it is defined as the *middle point* in a distribution. In Example 1, there are 11 scores. The middle score, with 50% on each side, is 81, which is the median. Thus, 81 is the value of the median for the set of scores. Note that there are five scores above 81 and five scores below 81.[2]

The *median* is the *middle point* in a distribution.

Example 1: Scores (arranged in order from low to high):

61, 61, 72, 77, 80, 81, 82, 85, 89, 90, 92

In Example 2, there are 6 scores. Because there is an even number of scores, the median is halfway between the two middle scores. To find the halfway point, sum the two middle scores (7 + 10 = 17) and divide by 2 (17/2 = 8.5). Thus, 8.5 is the value of the median of the set of scores in Example 2 below.

Example 2: Scores (arranged in order from low to high):

3, 3, 7, 10, 12, 15

An advantage of the *median* is that it is insensitive to extreme scores.[3] This is illustrated by Example 3, in which the extremely high score of 229 has no effect on the value of the median. The median is 8.5, which is the same value as in Example 2 above, despite the one extremely high score. Thus, the median is insensitive to the skew in a skewed distribution. Put another way, the median is an appropriate average for describing the typical participant in a highly skewed distribution.

The *median* is insensitive to extreme scores.

Example 3: Scores (arranged in order from low to high):

3, 3, 7, 10, 12, 229

The *mode* is another average. It is defined as the *most frequently occurring score*. In Example 4, the mode is 7 because it occurs more often than any other score.

The *mode* is the most *frequently occurring score.*

Example 4: Scores (arranged in order from low to high):

2, 2, 4, 6, 7, 7, 7, 9, 10, 12

A disadvantage of the mode is that there may be more than one mode for a given distribution. This is the case in Example 5 in which both 20 and 23 are modes.

Example 5: Scores (arranged in order from low to high):

17, 19, 20, 20, 22, 23, 23, 28

The following are guidelines for choosing among the three averages.

1. Other things being equal, choose the mean because more powerful statistical tests described later in this book can be applied to it than to the other averages. However, (a) the mean is *not* appropriate for describing highly skewed distributions, and (b) the mean is *not* appropriate for describing nominal and ordinal data. (See Section 4 to review these types of data.)

The *mean* is inappropriate for certain types of data.

2. Choose the *median* when the *mean* is inappropriate. The exception to this guideline is when describing nominal data. Nominal data (see Section 4) are naming data such as political affiliation, ethnicity, and so on. There is no natural order to these data; therefore, they cannot be put in order, which is required in order to calculate the median.

Choose the *median* when the *mean* is inappropriate, except when describing nominal data.

3. Choose the *mode* when an average is needed to describe nominal data. Note that when describing nominal data, it is often not necessary to use an average because percentages can be used as an alternative. For instance, if there are more registered Democrats than Republicans in a community, the best way to describe this is to report the percentage of people registered in each party. To state only that the modal political affiliation is Democratic (which is the mode in this example) is much less informative than reporting percentages.

Choose the *mode* as the average for nominal data. However, for nominal data, an average may not be needed.

Note that in a perfectly symmetrical distribution such as the normal distribution, the mean, median, and mode all have the same value. In skewed distributions, their values are different, as illustrated in Figure 9.1. In a distribution with a positive skew, the mean has the highest value because it is pulled in the direction of the extremely high scores. In a distribution with a negative skew, the mean has the lowest value because it is pulled in the direction of the extremely low scores. As noted earlier, the mean should not be used when a distribution is highly skewed.

In the normal distribution, the *mean*, *median*, and *mode* have the same value.

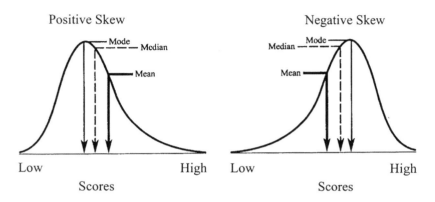

Figure 9.1. Positions of three averages in distributions with positive and negative skews.

When there is a positive skew, the *mean* is higher than the *median*.

When there is a negative skew, the *median* is higher than the *mean*.

Endnotes

[1] Another term for average is *measure of central tendency.*

[2] When there are tie scores in the middle, that is, when the middle score is earned by more than one participant, the method shown here for determining the median is only approximate and the result should be referred to as an *approximate median.*

[3] In Section 8, it was noted that the mean is pulled in the direction of extreme scores, which may make it a misleading average for skewed distributions.

Exercise for Section 9

Factual Questions

1. Which average always has 50% of the cases below it?

2. Which average is defined as the most frequently occurring score?

3. Which average is defined as the middle point in a distribution?

4. If you read that the median equals 42 on a test, what percentage of the participants have scores higher than 42?

5. What is the mode of the following scores? 11, 13, 16, 16, 18, 21, 25

6. Is the mean appropriate for describing highly skewed distributions?

7. This is a guideline from this section: "Choose the *median* when the *mean* is inappropriate." What is the exception to this guideline?

8. For describing nominal data, what is an alternative to reporting the mode?

9. In a distribution with a negative skew, does the "mean" *or* "median" have a higher value?

10. In a distribution with a positive skew, does the "mean" *or* "median" have a higher value?

Section 10

Range and Interquartile Range

Variability refers to differences among the scores of participants.[1] For instance, if all the participants who take a test earn the same score, there is no variability. In practice, of course, some variability (and often quite a large amount of variability) is usually found among participants in research studies.

A group of statistics called *measures of variability* are designed to concisely describe the amount of variability in a set of scores. In this section, two measures of variability (i.e., the range and interquartile range) are described. First, however, consider the importance of analyzing variability. This example illustrates the practical importance of variability:

> Suppose a new teacher is going to teach fourth grade next year and is offered a choice between two classes, both of which are very similar in terms of their average scores obtained on a standardized test. Before making a choice, the teacher would be wise to ask about the variability. He or she might learn, for instance, that one class has little variability (their scores are all very close to their average), while the other has tremendous variability (their scores vary from the highest to the lowest possible with a great deal of spread in between). Which class should the teacher choose? There is no right or wrong answer to the question, but clearly information on variability would be important in helping to make a decision.

A simple statistic that describes variability is the *range*, which is the difference between the highest score and the lowest score.[2] For the scores in Example 1, the range is 18 (20 minus 2). A researcher could report 18 as the range or simply state that the scores range from 2 to 20.

Example 1: Scores:

2, 5, 7, 7, 8, 8, l0, 12, 12, 15, 17, 20

Variability refers to differences among scores.

The *range* is the difference between the highest score and the lowest score.

45

A weakness of the range is that it is based on only the two most extreme scores, which may not accurately reflect the variability in the entire group. Consider Example 2. As in Example 1 on the previous page, the range in Example 2 is 18. However, there is much less variability among the participants than in Example 1. Notice that in Example 2, except for the one participant with a score of 20, all participants have scores in the narrow range from 2 to 6. Yet, the one participant in Example 2 with a score of 20 has pulled the range up to a value of 18, making it unrepresentative of the variability of the scores of the vast majority of the group.

Example 2: Scores:

2, 2, 2, 3, 4, 4, 5, 5, 5, 6, 6, 20

Scores such as the score 20 in Example 2 are known as *outliers*. They lie far outside the range of the vast majority of other scores and increase the size of the range. As a general rule, the range is inappropriate for describing a distribution of scores with outliers.

A better measure of variability is the *interquartile range* (*IQR*). It is defined as the range of the middle 50% of the participants. By using only the middle 50%, the range of the majority of the participants is being described and at the same time, outliers that could have an undue influence on the ordinary *range* are stripped of their influence.

Example 3 illustrates the meaning of the *interquartile range*. Notice that the scores are in order from low to high. The arrow on the left separates the lowest 25% from the middle 50%, and the arrow on the right separates the highest 25% from the middle 50%. It turns out that the range for the middle 50% is 3 points.[3] When 3.0 is reported as the *IQR*, consumers of research will know that the range of the middle 50% of participants is only 3 points, indicating little variability for the majority of the participants. Note that the undue influence of the outlier of 20 has been overcome by using the *interquartile range*.

Example 3: Scores:

2, 2, 2, 3, 4, 4, 5, 5, 5, 6, 6, 20
⇧   ⇧

A weakness of the range is that it is based only on the two most extreme scores.

Outliers are scores that lie far outside the range of the vast majority of other scores.

The *interquartile range* (*IQR*) is the range of the middle 50% of the participants.

The *IQR* is better than the *range* because it ignores outliers.

The interquartile range may be thought of as a first cousin of the *median*.[4] (To review the median, see Section 9.) Thus, when the *median* is reported as the average for a set of scores, it is customary to also report the *interquartile range* as the measure of variability.[5]

As a general rule, it is customary to report the value of an average (such as the value of the median) first, *followed by* the value of a measure of variability (such as the interquartile range).

> When the median is reported as the average, the *IQR* is usually reported for variability.

Endnotes

[1] Synonyms for variability are *spread* and *dispersion*.

[2] Some statisticians add the constant one (1) to the difference when computing the range.

[3] For those interested in the computation of the IQR, notice that the right arrow is at 5.5 and the left arrow is at 2.5. By subtracting (5.5 – 2.5 = 3.0), the approximate IQR is obtained.

[4] To calculate the median, count to the middle of the distribution. To calculate the IQR, count off the top and bottom quarters. This similarity in computations illustrates why they are cousins.

[5] The measure of variability that is associated with the mean is introduced in the next section. See the previous section for guidelines on when to report the median and the mean.

Exercise for Section 10

Factual Questions

1. What is the name of the group of statistics that are designed to concisely describe the amount of variability in a set of scores?

2. What are the two synonyms for *variability*?

3. If all participants have the same score on a test, what should be said about the variability in the set of scores?

4. If the differences among a set of scores are great, do we say that there is "much variability" *or* "little variability"?

5. What is the definition of the range?

6. What is a weakness of the range?

7. What is the outlier in the following set of scores?

   2, 31, 33, 35, 36, 38, 39

8. What is the outlier in the following set of scores?

   50, 50, 52, 53, 56, 57, 75

9. As a general rule, is the range appropriate for describing a distribution of scores with outliers?

10. What is the definition of the interquartile range?

11. Is the interquartile range unduly affected by outliers?

12. When the median is reported as the average, it is also customary to report which measure of variability?

Section 11

Standard Deviation

The *standard deviation* is the most frequently used *measure of variability*. In the previous section, you learned that the term *variability* refers to the differences among participants. Synonyms for *variability* are *spread* and *dispersion*.

The standard deviation is a statistic that provides an overall measurement of how much participants' scores differ from the *mean* score of their group. It is a special type of average of the deviations of the scores from their mean.[1]

The more spread out participants are around their mean, the larger the standard deviation. Comparison of Examples 1 and 2 illustrates this principle. Note that *S* is the symbol for the standard deviation.[2] Notice, too, that the mean is the same for both groups (i.e., *M* = 10.00 for each group), but Group A with the greater variability among the scores (*S* = 7.45) has a larger standard deviation than Group B (*S* = 1.49).

Example 1:

Scores for Group A: 0, 0, 5, 5, 10, 15, 15, 20, 20

M = 10.00, *S* = 7.45

Example 2:

Scores for Group B: 8, 8, 9, 9, 10, 11, 11, 12, 12

M = 10.00, *S* = 1.49

Now consider the scores of Group C in Example 3. All participants have the same score; therefore, there is no variability. When this is the case, the standard deviation equals zero, which indicates the complete lack of variability. Thus, *S* = 0.00.

Example 3:

Scores for Group C: 10, 10, 10, 10, 10, 10, 10, 10, 10, 10

M = 10.00, *S* = 0.00

Considering the three examples on the previous page, it is clear that the more participants differ from the mean of their group, the larger the standard deviation. Conversely, the less participants differ from the mean of their group, the smaller the standard deviation.

In review, even though the three groups in Examples 1, 2, and 3 on the previous page have the same mean, the following is true:

1. Group A has more variability than Groups B and C.

2. Group B has more variability than Group C.

3. Group C has no variability.

Thus, if you were reading a research report on the three groups, you would obtain important information about how the groups differ by considering their standard deviations.

The standard deviation takes on a special meaning when considered in relation to the normal curve (see Section 7 to review the normal curve) because the standard deviation was designed expressly to describe this curve. Here is a basic rule to remember: *About two-thirds of the cases (68%) lie within one standard deviation unit of the mean in a normal distribution.* (Note that "within one standard deviation unit" means one unit on *both* sides of the mean.)

About two-thirds of the cases lie within *one standard deviation unit* of the *mean* in a normal distribution.

Consider this example: Suppose that the mean of a set of normally distributed scores equals 70 and the standard deviation equals 10. Then, about two-thirds of the cases lie within 10 points of the mean. More precisely, 68% (a little more than two-thirds) of the cases lie within 10 points of the mean, which is illustrated in Figure 11.1. As you can see, 34% of the cases lie between a score of 60 and the mean of 70, while another 34% of the cases lie between the mean of 70 and a score of 80. In all, 68% of the cases lie between scores of 60 and 80.

More precisely, 68% (a bit more than two-thirds) lies within *one standard deviation unit* of the *mean.*

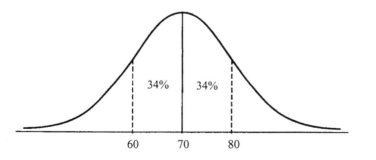

Figure 11.1. Normal curve with a standard deviation of 10.00.

The 68% rule applies to all normal curves. In fact, this is a property of the normal curve: 68% of the cases lie in the "middle area" bounded by one standard deviation on each side. Suppose, for instance, that for another group, the mean of their normal distribution also equals 70, but the group has less variability with a standard deviation of only 5, which is illustrated in Figure 11.2. As you can see, 68% of the cases still lie in the middle area of the distribution. However, because the standard deviation is only 5 points, 68% of the cases lie between scores of 65 and 75 for this group of participants.

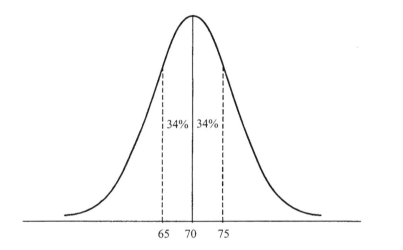

65   70   75

Figure 11.2. Normal curve with a standard deviation of 5.00.

The 68% guideline (sometimes called *the two-thirds rule of thumb*) strictly applies only to perfectly normal distributions. The less normal a distribution is, the less accurate the guideline is.

By examining Appendix A near the end of this book, you can see the calculation of the standard deviation is based on the differences between the mean and each of the scores in a distribution. Thus, the standard deviation can be thought of as the first cousin of the mean. As a result, when researchers report the mean (the most frequently used average), they usually also report the standard deviation immediately after reporting the mean. Example 4 shows a sentence in which both the means and standard deviations are reported.

When the *mean* is reported, the *standard deviation* is also usually reported.

Example 4:

Sample statement reporting means and standard deviations:

"Group A has a higher mean ($M = 67.89$, $S = 8.77$) than Group B ($M = 60.23$, $S = 8.54$)."

Endnotes

[1] Appendix A near the end of this book shows how to compute the standard deviation. By studying this appendix, you will learn what is meant by a "special type of average of the deviations."

[2] The uppercase, italicized letter *S* is the symbol for the standard deviation of a population. The lowercase, italicized letter *s* is the symbol for the standard deviation when only a sample of a population has been studied. Note that applied researchers sometimes use *S.D.* and *s.d.* as symbols for the standard deviation.

Exercise for Section 11

Factual Questions

1. The term "variability" refers to what?

2. Is the standard deviation a frequently used measure of variability?

3. The standard deviation provides an overall measurement of how much participants' scores differ from what other statistic?

4. If the differences among a set of scores are small, this indicates which of the following? (Circle one.)

   A. There is much variability.   B. There is little variability.

5. What is the symbol for the standard deviation when a population has been studied?

6. Will the scores for "Group D" *or* "Group E" below have a larger standard deviation if the two standard deviations are computed? (Do *not* compute the standard deviations; examine the scores to determine the answer.)

   Group D: 23, 23, 24, 25, 27, 27, 27

   Group E: 10, 19, 20, 21, 25, 30, 40

7. If all the participants in a group have the same score, what is the value of the standard deviation of the scores?

8. If you read the following statistics in a research report, which group should you conclude has the greatest variability?

   Group F: $M = 30.23$, $S = 2.14$

   Group G: $M = 25.99$, $S = 3.01$

   Group H: $M = 22.43$, $S = 4.79$

9. What percentage of the cases in a normal curve lies within one standard deviation unit of the mean (i.e., within one unit above *and* one unit below the mean)?

10. Suppose $M = 30$ and $S = 3$ for a normal distribution of scores. What percentage of the cases lies between scores of 27 and 30?

11. Suppose $M = 80$ and $S = 10$ for a normal distribution of scores. About 68% of the cases lies between what two scores?

Notes:

Part C

Correlational Statistics

Notes:

Section 12

Correlation

Correlation refers to the extent to which two variables are related across a group of participants. Consider scores on the College Entrance Examination Board's *Scholastic Aptitude Test* (*SAT*) and first-year GPA in college. Because the *SAT* is widely used as a predictor in college student selection, there should be a correlation between these scores and GPAs earned in college. Consider Example 1 in which *SAT-V* refers to the verbal portion of the *SAT*.[1] Notice that there is one group of students with two scores for each student. Is there a relationship between the two variables?

Example 1:

Student	*SAT-V*	GPA
John	333	1.0
Janet	756	3.8
Thomas	444	1.9
Scotty	629	3.2
Diana	501	2.3
Hillary	245	0.4

Indeed there is. Notice that students who scored high on the *SAT-V* such as Janet and Scotty had the highest GPAs. Also, those who scored low on the *SAT-V* such as Hillary and John had the lowest GPAs. This type of relationship is called a *direct relationship* (also called a *positive relationship*). In a direct relationship, those who score high on one variable tend to score high on the other *and* those who score low on one variable tend to score low on the other.

Example 2 on the next page also shows the scores on two variables for one group of participants. The first variable is self-concept, which was measured with 12 true–false items containing statements such as "I feel good about myself when I am in public." Participants earned one point for each statement that they marked as being true of them. Thus, the self-concept scores could range from zero (marking all statements as false) to 12 (marking all statements as true). Obviously, the higher a participant's score, the higher the self-concept. The second variable in Example 2 is depression measured with a standardized depression scale with possible scores from 20 to 80. Higher scores indicate more depression.

Do the data in Example 2 indicate that there is a relationship between self-concept and depression? Close examination indicates that there is a relationship. Notice that participants with high self-concept scores such as Sally and Jose (both with the highest possible self-concept score of 12) had relatively low depression scores of 25 and 29 (on a scale from 20 to 80). At the same time, participants with low self-concept scores such as Matt and Joan have high depression scores. In other words, those with high self-concepts tend to have low depression scores, while those with low self-concepts tend to have high depression scores. Such a relationship is called an *inverse relationship* (also called a *negative relationship*). In an inverse relationship, those who score high on one variable tend to score low on the other.

> In an *inverse* or *negative relationship*, those who score high on one variable tend to score low on the other.

Example 2:

Participant	Self-Concept	Depression
Sally	12	25
Jose	12	29
Sarah	10	38
Dick	7	50
Matt	8	61
Joan	4	72

It is important to note that just because a correlation between two variables is observed, it does not necessarily indicate that there is a *causal relationship* between the variables. In Example 2 above, for instance, the data do not establish whether (a) having a low self-concept causes depression or (b) being depressed causes an individual to have a low self-concept. In fact, there might not be any causal relationship at all between the two variables because a host of other variables (such as life circumstances, genetic depositions, and so on) might account for the relationship between self-concept and depression. For instance, having a disruptive home life might cause some individuals to have a low self-concept and at the same time cause

> Establishing a correlation does not necessarily establish a *causal relationship*.

these same individuals to become depressed.

In order to study *cause-and-effect*, a controlled *experiment* is needed in which different treatments are administered to the participants. (See Section 2 for a discussion of experiments.) For instance, to examine a possible causal link between self-concept and depression, a researcher could give an experimental group a treatment designed to improve self-concept and then compare the average level of depression of the experimental group with the average level of a control group.

In order to determine cause-and-effect, a controlled experiment is needed.

Although it is generally inappropriate to infer causality from a correlational study, such studies can still be of great value. For instance, the College Board is interested in how well the *SAT* works in predicting success in college. This can be revealed by examining the correlation between *SAT* scores and college GPAs. It is not necessary for the College Board to examine what causes high GPAs in an experiment for the purposes of determining the predictive validity of its test.

In addition to validating tests, correlations are of interest in developing theories. Often, a postulate of a theory may indicate that *X* should be related to *Y*. If a correlation is found in a correlational study, the finding helps to support the theory. If it is not found, it calls the theory into question.

Up to this point, only clear-cut examples have been considered. However, in practice, correlational data almost always include individuals who are exceptions to the overall trend, making the degree of correlation less obvious. Consider Example 3, which has the same students as in Example 1 but with the addition of two others: Joe and Patricia.

When large numbers of participants are examined, there are almost always exceptions to the trend.

Example 3:

Student	SAT-V	GPA
John	333	1.0
Janet	756	3.8
Thomas	444	1.9
Scotty	629	3.2
Diana	501	2.3
Hillary	245	0.4
Joe	630	0.9
Patricia	404	3.1

Joe has a high *SAT-V* score but a very low GPA. Thus, Joe is an *exception* to the rule that high values on one variable are associated with high values on the other. There may be a variety of explanations for this exception: Joe may have had a family crisis during his first year in college *or* he may have abandoned his good work habits to make time for TV viewing and campus parties as soon as he moved away from home to college. Patricia is another exception: Perhaps she made an extra effort to apply herself to college work, which could not be predicted by the *SAT*. When studying hundreds of participants, there will be many exceptions, some large and some small. To make sense of such data, statistical techniques are required. These will be explored in the next four sections.

To make sense of data with many exceptions, statistical techniques are required.

Endnote

[1]*SAT-V* scores range from 200 to 800.

Exercise for Section 12

Factual Questions

1. A direct relationship was found between scores on a reading test and a vocabulary test. This indicates that those who scored high on the reading test tended to have what kind of score on the vocabulary test?

   A. A high score.   B. A low score.

2. What is another name for an inverse relationship?

3. Is the relationship between the scores on Test A and Test B "direct" *or* "inverse"?

Participant	Test A	Test B
David	20	600
Julie	30	500
Happy	40	400
Shorty	50	300
Marcia	60	200
Kelly	70	100

4. Is the relationship between the scores on Test C and Test D "direct" *or* "inverse"?

Participant	Test C	Test D
Monica	1	33
Lola	2	38
Jim	4	40
Oscar	6	45
Joey	8	52
Cathleen	9	57

5. There is a positive relationship between the scores on Tests E and F. Which participant is an exception to the rule? Explain why he or she is an exception.

Participant	Test E	Test F
Homer	1050	160
Billy	2508	169
Scott	2702	184
Kathy	3040	205
Leona	5508	90
Bruce	5567	210

6. In an inverse relationship, those who tend to score high on one variable tend to have what kind of score on the other variable?

7. In an inverse relationship, those who tend to score low on one variable tend to have what kind of score on the other variable?

8. What type of study is needed in order to identify *cause-and-effect* relationships?

9. Is *correlation* a good way to determine *cause-and-effect*?

10. When a large number of cases are examined and a positive relationship is found, what else should one expect to find?

Questions for Discussion

11. Name two variables that you think have a direct relationship with each other.

12. Name two variables that you think have an inverse relationship with each other.

Section 13

Pearson *r*

A statistician named Karl Pearson developed a very widely used statistic for describing the relationship between two variables (see Section 12 for a discussion of the correlation between two variables). The symbol for Pearson's statistic is a lowercase, italicized letter *r*, and it is often called the Pearson *r*. Its full, formal name is the *Pearson product-moment correlation coefficient*, and there are variations on the name in research literature such as the *Pearson correlation coefficient* or the *product-moment correlation coefficient*. These are some of the basic properties of the Pearson *r*:

1. It can range only from −1.00 to 1.00.

2. −1.00 indicates a perfect inverse relationship, which is the strongest possible inverse relationship.

3. 1.00 indicates a perfect direct relationship, which is the strongest possible direct relationship.

4. 0.00 indicates the complete absence of a relationship.

5. The closer a value is to 0.00, the weaker the relationship.

6. The closer a value is to −1.00 or 1.00, the stronger it is.

This is a graphic representation of the properties:

−1.00				0.00				1.00
⇧	⇧	⇧	⇧	⇧	⇧	⇧	⇧	⇧
perfect	strong	moderate	weak	none	weak	moderate	strong	perfect

Notice the labels *strong*, *moderate*, and *weak* are used in conjunction with both positive and negative values of the Pearson *r*. Also, note that exact numerical values are not given for these labels. This is because the interpretation and labeling of an *r* may vary from one investigator to another and from one type of investigation to another. For instance, one way to examine *test reliability* is to administer the same test twice to a group of participants without trying to change the participants between administrations of the test. This will result in two scores per examinee, which can be correlated using the

The full name of the Pearson r is Pearson product-moment correlation coefficient.

A Pearson r ranges from −1.00 to 1.00.

Both −1.00 and 1.00 indicate a perfect relationship.

A value of 0.00 indicates the complete absence of a relationship.

The interpretation of a Pearson r varies, depending on the type of study.

Pearson *r*. In such a study, a professionally constructed test should yield high values of *r* such as .75 or higher.[1] A result such as .65 probably would be characterized as only moderately strong. In another type of study, where high values of *r* are seldom achieved (such as predicting college GPAs from College Board scores earned a year earlier), a value of *r* of .65 might be interpreted as strong or even very strong.[2]

The interpretation of the values of *r* is further complicated by the fact that an *r* is *not a proportion*. Thus, for instance, it follows that multiplying .50 by 100 does *not* yield a percentage. In other words, .50 is *not* equivalent to 50%. This is important because we are used to thinking of .50 as being halfway between 0.00 and 1.00. Yet, on Karl Pearson's scale for *r*, .50 is *not* halfway between 0.00 and 1.00. This problem in interpretation is explored further in Section 14. In that section, you will learn about a statistic that is based on *r* and that may be interpreted as a proportion (convertible to a percentage).

Appendix B near the end of this book contains some additional notes on the interpretation of values of *r*.

An *r* is not a *proportion*. Thus, multiplying it by 100 does *not* yield a percentage.

Endnotes

[1] A test is said to be reliable if its results are consistent. For example, if you measured the length of a table twice with a tape measure, you would expect very similar results both times—unless your measurement technique was unreliable.

[2] Careful study of the literature on the topic being investigated is needed in order to arrive at a non-numerical label or interpretation of a Pearson *r* that will be accepted by other researchers.

Exercise for Section 13

Factual Questions

1. What is the full, formal name of the Pearson *r*?

2. What does a Pearson *r* of 0.00 indicate?

3. What does a Pearson *r* of −1.00 indicate?

4. Which one of the following indicates the strongest relationship?

   A. .68   B. .77   C. −.98   D. .50

5. Are inverse relationships always weak?

6. Which one of the following indicates the weakest relationship?

    A. .93 B. −.88 C. −.95 D. .21

7. Is it possible for a relationship to be both direct and weak?

8. Is it possible for a relationship to be both inverse and strong?

9. Consider a value of *r* of .65. According to this section, would it always be appropriate to characterize the relationship as being "very strong"?

10. Consider a value of *r* of .50. Would it be appropriate to multiply this value by 100 and to interpret it as representing 50%?

Question for Discussion

11. Very briefly describe a study you might conduct in which it would be appropriate to compute a Pearson *r* (i.e., a study with one group of participants with two scores per participant). Predict whether the *r* would be "positive" *or* "negative" and whether it would be "high" *or* "low" in value.

Notes:

Section 14

Coefficient of Determination

The *coefficient of determination* is useful when interpreting a Pearson *r*. Its symbol, r^2, explains how it is computed; to obtain it, simply square *r*. Thus, for a Pearson *r* of .60, r^2 equals .36 (.60 × .60 = .36).

Although the computation is simple, the meaning of r^2 is sometimes difficult to grasp at first. Let us begin by considering the scores in Example 1. Five young children took an oral vocabulary knowledge test before they began learning how to read. After six months of instruction, they took a reading test. As you can see, there is a positive relationship because those who are low on vocabulary (such as John) are also low on reading *and* those who are high on vocabulary (such as Diana) are also high on reading. Thus, we can say that the vocabulary scores are predictive of the subsequent reading scores. But how predictive?

Example 1:

Student	Oral Vocabulary	Reading
John	3	6
Janet	5	8
Thomas	4	9
Scotty	9	10
Diana	10	12

As it turns out, the value of the Pearson *r* for the relationship between the two sets of scores in Example 1 is .90.[1] Thus, we can say that the oral vocabulary scores are highly predictive of reading scores. However, it is possible to be more precise than saying "highly predictive" by using the coefficient of determination. Let us consider how to be more precise.

First, notice that there are differences among the scores on the oral vocabulary test in Example 1. These differences are referred to as *variance*. There is also variance in the scores on the reading test. When interpreting a Pearson *r*, an important question is: *What percentage of the variance on one variable is accounted for by the vari-*

To obtain the *coefficient of determination*, square *r*.

The *coefficient of determination*, when converted to a percentage, indicates how much variance on one variable is accounted for by the variance on the other.

67

ance on the other? If we are trying to predict reading scores from oral vocabulary scores, the question might be phrased as: *What percentage of the variance in reading scores is predicted by the variance in vocabulary scores?* The answer to the question is easily determined. Simply square r and multiply it by 100. For the scores shown in Example 1, $r = .90$. Thus,

$$.90 \times .90 = .81 \times 100 = 81\%$$

We have determined that 81% (*not* 90%) of the variance on one variable is accounted for by the variance on the other in this example.[2]

Let us put the 81% in perspective. Suppose we are trying to predict how students will score in reading. Suppose we naively put all the students' names on slips of paper in a hat and draw a name and declare that the first name drawn will probably perform best on the reading test, and draw a second name and declare that this person will probably perform second best on the reading test, and so on. What percentage of the variance in reading will we predict using this procedure? In the long run with large numbers of students, the answer is about zero (0.00) percent. In the above example, the differences (i.e., variance) in oral vocabulary accounted for 81% of the differences (i.e., variance) in reading, which is 81% better than using a random process to make predictions.[3]

It follows, however, that if we can account for 81% of the variance, 19% (100% − 81% = 19%) of the variance is *not* accounted for. Thus, we are 19% of the way from reaching perfection in the ability to predict reading achievement.

Table 14.1 on the next page shows selected values of r, the corresponding values of r^2, and the percentage of variance accounted for and not accounted for. Notice that small values of r shrink dramatically when converted to r^2, indicating that we should be very cautious when interpreting small values of r because they are much further from perfection than they might seem at first.[4]

If you are having difficulty understanding the coefficient of determination, consider again what Table 14.1 tells us. When $r = .10$, our ability to predict is 1% better than no ability to predict; when $r = .20$, our ability to predict is 4% better than no ability to predict, and so on. Thus, the coefficient of determination, when converted to a percentage, tells us how effective one variable is in predicting another

A percentage may be obtained by multiplying r^2 by 100.

If you draw names at random, your ability to predict is zero percent.

If $r = .90$, the ability to predict is 81% better than zero.

Small values of r shrink dramatically when squared.

expressed in terms of percentages.

Table 14.1
Selected values of r and r²

r	r²	% accounted for	% *not* accounted for
.10	.01	1%	99%
.20	.04	4%	96%
.30	.09	9%	91%
.40	.16	16%	84%
.50	.25	25%	75%
.60	.36	36%	64%
.70	.49	49%	51%
.80	.64	64%	36%
.90	.81	81%	19%
1.00	1.00	100%	0%

Keeping Table 14.1 in mind when reading research articles should give you pause because many authors interpret values of r in the .20 to .40 range as indicating important relationships. In fact, they may be of some practical importance under certain circumstances. However, keep in mind that in this range 84% to 96% of the variance on one variable is *not* accounted for by the other. When considering a prediction study, an r of .40 (with variance accounted for of only 16%) leaves much room for improvement when attempting to predict one variable from another.

When the values of r are less than .40, more than 84% of the variance is *not* accounted for.

Endnotes

[1] Computational procedures for obtaining the value of a Pearson r are beyond the scope of this book. In this example, r does not equal 1.00 because there are exceptions to the positive trend; notice that although Janet is higher than Thomas on vocabulary, she is lower than Thomas on reading.

[2] *Variance accounted for* is sometimes called *explained variance*.

[3] In practice, standardized reading readiness tests designed to predict first-grade reading ability account for only about a third of the variance in reading ability.

[4] Note that if there is no variance on either variable, the Pearson r will equal 0.00, and $r²$ will also equal 0.00.

Exercise for Section 14

Factual Questions

1. For a given value of r, how is the value of the coefficient of determination computed?

2. What is the symbol for the coefficient of determination?

3. When $r = .50$, what is the value of the coefficient of determination?

4. When $r = .50$, what percentage of the variance on one variable is accounted for by the variance on the other?

5. When $r = .50$, what percentage of the variance on one variable is *not* accounted for by the variance on the other?

6. When $r = .30$, what percentage of the variance on one variable is accounted for by the variance on the other?

7. When $r = .30$, what percentage of the variance on one variable is *not* accounted for by the variance on the other?

8. Do "large values" *or* "small values" of r shrink more dramatically when squared?

9. When the Pearson $r = .40$, is the percentage accounted for equal to 40%? Explain.

Section 15

Scattergram

The general term "correlation" refers to the extent to which two variables are related across a group of participants. The concept of correlation is described in Section 12. Then, the Pearson r is described in Section 13, and the coefficient of determination (r^2), which is used to interpret values of the Pearson r, is described in Section 14.

The Pearson r is a statistic that concisely describes the degree of correlation between two variables, using a single numerical value to describe it. A *scattergram* (also known as a *scatter diagram*) is a statistical figure (i.e., a drawing) that illustrates the correlation between two variables.

While scattergrams are seldom presented in research reports, by studying the scattergrams in this section of this book, you will gain a better understanding of the meanings of the values of r and r^2. To this end, for each scattergram shown below, the associated values of r and r^2 are shown.

Consider the scores in Example 1, which shows scores on a basic math test taken before students enrolled in an algebra class and the grades the students subsequently earned in the algebra class. In Example 1 below, 4.0 = A, 3.5 = A–, 3.0 = B, and so on.

Example 1:

Student	Math Score	Algebra Grade
Joey	4	1.0
June	6	1.5
Justin	8	2.0
Jill	10	2.5
Janice	12	3.0
Jake	14	3.5
Jude	16	4.0

Notice that the relationship in Example 1 is clearly direct (i.e., positive). Joey has the lowest math score *and* the lowest algebra grade, June has the next-lowest math score *and* the next-lowest algebra grade, and so on without exception. In fact, the relationship is perfect, so $r = 1.00$, and r^2 also equals 1.00 (i.e., $1.00 \times 1.00 = 1.00$). As discussed in Section 14, the values of r^2 can be converted to percentages by multiplying by 100. Doing so for an r^2 of 1.00 yields 100%. Thus, we can say that 100% of the variance in the algebra grades is accounted for by the variance in the math scores. (See Section 14 to review the concept of "variance accounted for.") Put in everyday terms, we can say that the data in Example 1 on the previous page indicate that the basic math scores are a perfect predictor of subsequent algebra grades.

Figure 1 shows the scattergram for the scores in Example 1 on the previous page. Each dot on the scattergram represents the *two* scores for one student. For instance, the dot for Justin shows that he had a score of 8 on the math test and a grade of 2.0 (i.e., a grade of "C") in the algebra class.

Because the relationship is perfect, the dots in Figure 1 follow a single straight line. In addition, because the relationship is direct (i.e., positive), the dots go from the lower-left corner to the upper-right corner.

When a relationship is perfect, the dots follow a single straight line from the lower left to the upper right.

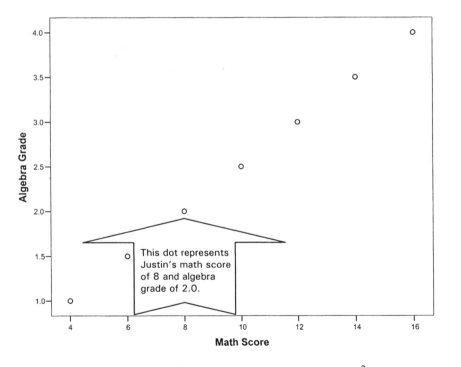

Figure 1. Perfect, direct relationship ($r = 1.00$, $r^2 = 1.00$, percent explained variance = 100%).

Perfect relationships are seldom found in the social and behavioral sciences. For instance, in practice, the relationship between math scores and subsequent algebra grades is usually far from perfect because different students have different areas of strength (such as a student being strong in basic math) and weakness (such as the same student being weak in comprehending abstractions in algebra).

Example 2 below is the same as Example 1 on page 71 except that Mike's math score and algebra grade have been added; these are shown in bold in Example 2 below. Notice that while Mike is near the bottom in math, he is about in the middle of the group in algebra.

Example 2:

Student	Math Score	Algebra Grade
Mike	**5**	**3.0**
Joey	4	1.0
June	6	1.5
Justin	8	2.0
Jill	10	2.5
Janice	12	3.0
Jake	14	3.5
Jude	16	4.0

As it turns out, for the data in Example 2 above, the value of r is .83, which indicates that the relationship is strong (it applies to all students except Mike), but it is not perfect (because of Mike).

The scattergram in Figure 2 on the next page is for the relationship between the scores in Example 2 above. Notice that the overall trend clearly shows that the relationship is direct. However, Mike's two scores are an exception, creating a dot that is off the line created by the other dots. Because of Mike's scores, the value of r is now only .83 (instead of 1.00 in Example 1 on page 71, which does not include Mike), with a corresponding value of r^2 of .69 (for 69% explained variance).

Perfect relationships are rare.

In Example 2, Mike is an exception to the overall trend.

Because of Mike, the relationship is no longer perfect.

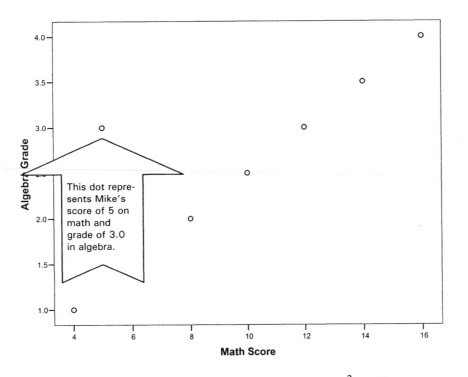

Figure 2. Strong, direct relationship ($r = .83$, $r^2 = .69$, percent explained variance = 69%).

When correlating cognitive variables such as math test scores and algebra grades, there will be many exceptions to the trend. Example 3 shows the same scores as in Example 2 on the previous page with additional students added, each of whom deviates somewhat from the overall trend that indicates a direct relationship. The scores of the additional students are shown in bold in Example 3.

Example 3:

Student	Math Score	Algebra Grade
Martin	**13**	**2.0**
Mitch	**11**	**1.5**
Mary	**10**	**2.0**
Michelle	**6**	**1.5**
Manny	**3**	**2.0**
Mike	5	3.0
Joey	4	1.0
June	6	1.5
Justin	8	2.0

Continued →

74

Example 3 continued

Jill	10	2.5
Janice	12	3.0
Jake	14	3.5
Jude	16	4.0

The scattergram in Figure 3 is for the relationship between the scores in Example 3. Notice that the overall trend still shows that the relationship is direct (i.e., the dots generally follow a pattern from the lower left to the upper right). However, there is a scattering of dots that indicates deviations from the overall trend. Because of the scatter, r is now only .64 (instead of 1.00 in Figure 1 on page 72 and .83 in Figure 2 on the previous page). The corresponding value of r^2 for an r of .64 is .41 (for 41% explained variance). Put in everyday terms, the data in Example 3 indicate that the math test is 41% better than zero in the ability to predict algebra grades. Correspondingly, 59% of the variance in algebra grades is unpredicted by the math scores (100% − 41% = 59%).

Because of the scatter in Figure 3, the relationship is not perfect.

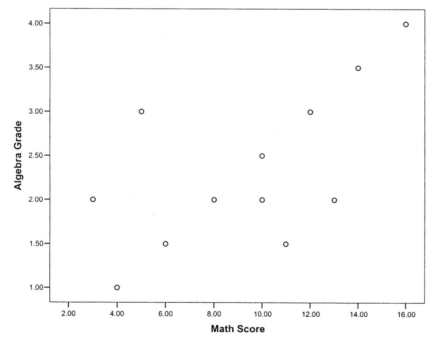

Figure 3. Moderately strong, direct relationship (r = .64, r^2 = .41, percent explained variance = 41%).

As you know from previous sections, sometimes relationships are inverse (i.e., negative). Example 4 on the next page shows scores on the variables of cheerfulness and depression. Cheerfulness was measured with statements such as "Most mornings when I wake up, I feel cheerful," while depression was measured with statements such as "I often feel blue on my way to work." Participants responded on a scale from Strongly Agree to Strongly Disagree to the statements. Summing their responses across the items, participants could earn scores ranging from zero (marking "strongly disagree" to all items) to 30 (marking "strongly agree" to all items) on each variable.

Examination of the scores in Example 4 suggests an inverse (i.e., negative) relationship. For instance, Blair and Leslie have the *highest* cheerfulness scores, but they have the *lowest* depression scores. At the same time, Hilda and Oscar have the *lowest* cheerfulness scores, but they have the *highest* depression scores. Thus, those who are high on cheerfulness tend to be low on depression, while those who are low on cheerfulness tend to be high on depression.

However, there are exceptions to the overall inverse trend. For instance, while Zeus and Blondie have the same cheerfulness scores (each has a score of 20), Zeus has a much higher depression score (a score of 24) than Blondie (a score of 8). These and other exceptions to the inverse trend make the relationship less than perfect, which is illustrated in Figure 4, which is the scattergram for the data in Example 4.

Example 4 shows scores with an inverse relationship.

Example 4:

Student	Cheerfulness Score	Depression Score
Blair	30	4
Leslie	27	5
Homer	24	7
Zeus	20	24
Blondie	20	8
Suzanne	18	10
Rachel	16	10
Brett	14	14
Wendy	13	9
Alistair	11	12
Steve	9	23
Hilda	6	29
Oscar	0	30

The scattergram in Figure 4 is for the relationship between the scores in Example 4. Notice that the overall trend shows that the relationship is inverse (i.e., the dots generally follow a pattern from the upper left to the lower right). However, there is a scattering of dots that indicates that the relationship is not perfect. The value of r for the relationship in Figure 4 is –.79. The corresponding value of r^2 for an r of –.79 is .62 (for 62% explained variance).[1] Put in everyday terms, the data in Example 4 indicate that the cheerfulness scores are 62% better than zero in the ability to predict depression scores. Correspondingly, 38% of the variance in depression scores is unpredicted by the cheerfulness scores (100% – 62% = 38%).

In Figure 4, the pattern from the upper left to the lower right indicates a negative relationship.

The scattering of dots in Figure 4 indicates that the inverse relationship is not perfect.

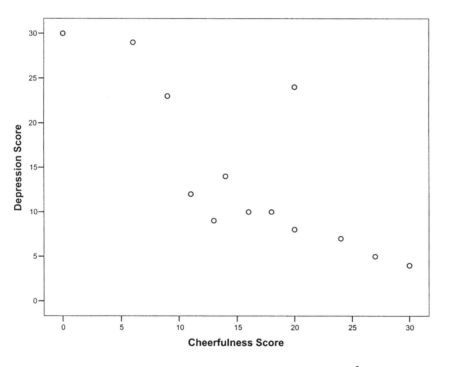

Figure 4. Strong, inverse relationship ($r = -.79$, $r^2 = .62$, percent explained variance = 62%).

Summary

As you can see from the scattergrams in this section, the following is true:

• When the dots form a pattern that goes from the *lower left* to the *upper right*, the relationship is *direct* (i.e., positive).

- When the dots form a pattern that goes from the *upper left* to the *lower right*, the relationship is *inverse* (i.e., positive).

- When the dots perfectly follow a single straight line, the relationship is perfect.

- The greater the amount of scatter around the line, the weaker the relationship.

Endnote

[1] Notice that although the value of r is negative, the value of r^2 is positive. When multiplying a negative by a negative (as in squaring a negative), the product is positive. Thus, to determine whether a relationship is negative or positive, the value of r must be examined (or the scattergram must be examined). To interpret the strength of *either* a positive or negative value of r, the value of r^2, which is always positive, should be examined.

Exercise for Section 15

Factual Questions

1. What is the general term that refers to the extent to which two variables are related across one group of participants?

2. While scattergrams are seldom presented in research reports, they are useful for obtaining what?

3. In Example 1, Jude and Jake have the two highest math scores *and* the two highest algebra grades. This suggests that the relationship is (circle one)

   A. direct.   B. inverse.

4. "The more scattered the dots are in a scattergram, the stronger the relationship." This statement is (circle one)

   A. true.   B. false.

5. When a relationship is perfect, what is the percentage of explained variance?

6. "Perfect relationships are frequently found in the social and behavioral sciences." This statement is (circle one)

   A. true.   B. false.

7. Which of the four scattergrams in this section has the greatest amount of scatter?

8. When the dots on a scattergram form a pattern going from the upper left to the lower right, what type of relationship is indicated?

Question for Discussion

9. To what extent do the scattergrams in this section and the discussion of them help you understand the concept of correlation and the meanings of various values of the Pearson r? Explain.

Notes:

Section 16

Multiple Correlation

In Sections 12, 13, 14, and 15, the correlation between only two variables was considered. In this section, the correlation between the combination of two variables with a third variable is explored.

This section concerns the correlation between the combination of two variables with a third variable.

To understand the topic of this section, consider the three sets of scores in Example 1 on the next page. The scores on a basic math test taken before students enrolled in an algebra class and the algebra grades are the same scores as in Example 3 on pages 74 to 75 in Section 15, except that they have been rearranged according to algebra grade with the highest grade of 4.0 at the top.

As you know from Figure 3 on page 75 in Section 15, $r = .64$ for the relationship between the basic math test scores and subsequent algebra grades, indicating that the math scores are a moderately good predictor of subsequent algebra grades. As you also know, the corresponding value of r^2 is .41 (for 41% explained variance). In everyday terms, this means that 59% of the differences in algebra grades remain *unpredicted* by the basic math test.

Because so much of the variance in algebra grades is not predicted by the basic math test, it would be desirable to add an additional predictor variable to determine if the degree of prediction could be improved by using two predictors (instead of using only the basic math scores). To this end, scores on an attitude toward math scale have been added as a potential additional predictor. Attitude toward math was measured before enrollment in an algebra class. The attitude scale had 15 items with possible scores ranging from zero to 20.

The ability to predict might be improved by using two predictors instead of only one.

Inspection of the attitude toward math scores and the algebra grades in Example 1 on the next page suggests that there is a direct correlation. For instance, Jude has the highest algebra grade (4.0) and also has the highest attitude toward math score (20). In contrast, Joey has the lowest algebra grade (1.0) and also has the lowest attitude toward math score (3). When high scores on one variable are associated with high scores on the other variable (and when low scores on one are associated with low scores on the other), we know that the relationship is direct (i.e., positive).

Example 1: Scores for 13 Students Arranged According to
Algebra Grades

Student	Math Score	Attitude Toward Math	Algebra Grade
Jude	16	20	4.0
Jake	14	13	3.5
Janice	12	12	3.0
Mike	5	11	3.0
Jill	10	7	2.5
Martin	13	9	2.0
Manny	3	9	2.0
Mary	10	6	2.0
Justin	8	14	2.0
Mitch	11	8	1.5
Michelle	6	12	1.5
June	6	12	1.5
Joey	4	3	1.0

Inspection of the attitude toward math scores and the algebra grades in Example 1 also suggests that the relationship is not perfect. For instance, Justin has a relatively high attitude toward math score (14) but a grade of only 2.0 in algebra class. Also, Michelle has a relatively high attitude toward math score (12) but a grade of only 1.5 in algebra. These and other exceptions indicate the need to calculate the value of the Pearson r for these data to obtain a concise description of the degree of correlation. As it turns out, the Pearson r for this relationship is .68, suggesting that attitude toward math is a good predictor of success in algebra.

In review, this is what is known about the ability to predict algebra grades based on the data in Example 1:

- For the relationship between basic math scores and algebra grades, $r = .64$.

- For the relationship between attitude toward math scores and algebra grades, $r = .68$.

Given these relationships, it seems likely that if we use a combination of *both* basic math scores *and* attitude toward math scores to predict algebra grades, a researcher could improve the abil-

Using a combination of two sets of scores might improve the ability to predict.

ity to predict algebra grades over using just one of the predictors.

To determine the degree of relationship between a combination of the two predictors (basic math scores and attitude toward math scores) to predict algebra grades, a *multiple correlation coefficient,* whose symbol is an uppercase, italicized *R*, can be calculated. While the calculation of statistics is beyond the scope of this book, it turns out that for the data in Example 1, *R* = .77, which is higher than only basic math scores with an *r* of .64 or only attitude toward math scores with an *r* of .68.

A multiple correlation coefficient has the same basic characteristics as *r*. Specifically, the closer the value of *R* is to zero, the weaker the relationship. For an inverse relationship, the closer *R* is to –1.00, the stronger the relationship. For a direct relationship, the closer *R* is to 1.00, the stronger the relationship. Thus, we can say that *R* = .77 represents a relatively strong, direct relationship because it is fairly close to 1.00.

As you know from Section 14, the coefficient of determination for a value of the Pearson *r* can be calculated by squaring *r*. Multiplying the square of *r* by 100% gives the percentage of variance on one variable accounted for by the other variable. The same holds true for *R*. For the value of *R* of .77 for the data in Example 1, R^2 = .59 (i.e., .77 × .77 = .59). Multiplying .59 by 100% indicates that 59% of the variance in algebra grades is accounted for by the combination of basic math test scores and attitude toward math scores.

Here is a summary of what is now known about the data in Example 1:

- The single best predictor of algebra grades is attitude toward math scores (*r* = .68, r^2 = .46 for 46% variance accounted for).

- The next best predictor of algebra grades is basic math test scores (*r* = .64, r^2 = .41 for 41% variance accounted for).

- If *both* attitude toward math scores and basic math test scores are used *in combination,* the degree of prediction is greater than for either of the two individual predictors (*R* = .77, R^2 = .59 for 59% variance accounted for).

Clearly, then, for predicting algebra grades, it would be better to use a combination of the attitude toward math scores and basic math test scores.[1]

The symbol for a *multiple correlation coefficient* is an uppercase, italicized *R*.

A *multiple correlation coefficient* has the same basic characteristics as *r*.

R^2 multiplied by 100% indicates the percentage of variance on one variable accounted for by the combination of predictors.

Note that multiple correlation coefficients can be calculated for a combination of more than two predictors. For instance, it is common to determine the validity of college admissions procedures by calculating the value of *R* for a combination of at least three predictors, such as (1) verbal college admissions test scores, (2) quantitative college admissions test scores, and (3) high school grades, using freshman grades in college as the variable being predicted.

> A *multiple correlation coefficient* can be calculated for a combination of more than two predictors.

Endnote

[1] The value of *R* is for the best possible combination of the scores on the predictor variables. The statistical methods for determining the best possible combination are beyond the scope of this book.

Exercise for Section 16

Factual Questions

1. Inspection (without any computations) of the attitude toward math scores and the algebra grades in Example 1 suggests that the correlation is (circle one)

   A. direct. B. inverse.

2. Inspection (without any computations) of the attitude toward math scores and the algebra grades in Example 1 suggests that the correlation is (circle one)

   A. perfect. B. not perfect.

3. In the example in this section, which of the following is the single best predictor of algebra grades? (Circle one.)

   A. Basic math scores. B. Attitude toward math scores.

4. Which of the following values of *R* represents the strongest relationship? (Circle one.)

   A. $R = .45$ B. $R = .12$ C. $R = -.66$

5. Suppose a researcher found a value of *R* of .40 for predicting the scores on variable Y from variables X and Z. Expressed as a percentage, what is the amount of variance in variable Y accounted for by the variance in the combination of variables X and Z?

6. Suppose a researcher is examining the validity of a combination of the length of engagement and the number of hours in premarital counseling as predictors of subsequent marital satisfaction. Which correlational statistic should the researcher compute for this research problem? (Circle one.)

   A. r. B. R.

7. Suppose a researcher is examining the validity of a set of scores on an oral language test to predict a set of scores that first-graders earn on a beginning reading test. Which correlational statistic should the researcher compute for this research problem? (Circle one.)

   A. r. B. R.

8. Can multiple correlation coefficients be calculated for a combination of more than two predictors?

Question for Discussion

9. Examine Example 1 on page 82. Michelle has the fourth-highest attitude toward math score (a score of 12). However, she has an algebra grade near the bottom of the group (a grade of 1.5). What does this one case tell you about the relationship between attitude toward math and algebra grades? (Keep in mind that the overall relationship is direct.)

Notes:

Part D

Inferential Statistics

Notes:

Section 17

Variations on Random Sampling

As noted in Section 3, a *population* consists of all members of the group of interest to a researcher. A population may be small, such as all social workers employed by a public hospital in Detroit, or it may be large, such as all social workers in Michigan. The larger a population, the more likely a researcher will study only a sample of the population and *infer* that what is true of the sample is also true of the population.[1] The process of making such an inference is referred to by statisticians as *generalizing* from a sample to a population.

Freedom from bias is the most important characteristic of a sample.[2] An unbiased sample is defined as one in which all individuals in a population have an equal chance of being included as a participant. The basic method for obtaining an unbiased sample is to use *random sampling* from a population. Various types of random sampling are described below.

Random sampling yields an unbiased sample.

To draw a *simple random sample*, a researcher can put names on slips of paper and draw the number needed for the sample. This method is efficient for drawing samples from small populations.

Names can be drawn to obtain a random sample.

To draw a simple random sample from a large population, it is more efficient to use a *table of random numbers* than to write names on slips of paper. A portion of a table of random numbers is shown in Appendix C near the end of this book.[3] In this table, there is no sequence to the numbers and in a large table of random numbers, each number appears about the same number of times. To use the table, first assign everyone in the population a *number name*. For instance, if there are 90 individuals in a population, name the first individual 01, the second individual 02, the third individual 03, etc., until you reach the last individual, whose number is 90.[4] (Often, computerized records have the individuals already numbered, which simplifies the process. Any set of numbers will work as number names as long as each individual has a different number and all individuals have the same number of digits in their number names.) To use the table, flip to any page in a book of random numbers and put your finger on the page without looking. This will determine the starting point. Let us

A *table of random numbers* may also be used to draw a random sample.

To use a *table of random numbers*, give each person in the population a *number name*.

start in the upper left-hand corner of the table in Appendix C for the sake of illustration. Because each individual has a two-digit number name, the first two digits identify the first participant; this is individual number 21. The next two digits to the right are 0 and 4; thus, individual number 04 will also be included in the sample. The third number is 98. Because there are only 90 in the population, skip 98 and continue to the right to 08, which is the number of the next individual drawn. Continue moving across the rows to select the sample.

Stratified random sampling is usually superior to simple random sampling. In stratified random sampling, the population is first divided into strata that are believed to be relevant to the variable(s) being studied. Suppose, for instance, you wanted to survey opinions on alcohol consumption with all students on a college campus as the population. If you suspect that men and women might differ in their opinions on alcohol consumption, it would be desirable to first stratify the population according to gender and then draw separately from each stratum at random. Specifically, you would draw a random sample of men and then separately draw a random sample of women. The same percentage should be drawn from each stratum. For instance, if you want to sample 10% of the population and there are 1,600 men and 2,000 women, you would draw 160 men and 200 women. Notice that there are more women in the sample than men, which is appropriate because the women are more numerous in the population. It is important to note that you would *not* be stratifying in order to compare men with women. Rather, the purpose of stratifying is to obtain a single sample of the college population that is representative in terms of gender.[5]

> In *stratified random sampling*, draw participants at random separately from each stratum.

> Draw the same percentage, not the same number, from each stratum.

In the stratified random sample being considered, the benefits of randomization (i.e., the elimination of bias) have been retained. In addition, you have gained the advantage of having appropriate proportions of men and women in the sample. If your hunch was correct that men and women differ in their opinions on alcohol consumption, you would have increased the precision of the results by stratifying.[6]

Note that stratifying does not eliminate all sampling errors. For instance, when you drew the women at random, you may have by chance obtained women for the sample that are not representative of all women on the campus; the same, of course, holds true for men. Nevertheless, stratifying has eliminated the possibility of obtaining a disproportionately large number of either men or women for the sample (i.e., it eliminates a particular *type* of sampling error—*not* all sampling errors).

For large-scale studies, *multistage random sampling* may be used. In this technique, a researcher might do the following. Stage 1: draw a sample of counties at random from all counties in a state; Stage 2: draw a sample of voting precincts at random from all precincts in the counties previously selected; and Stage 3: draw individual voters at random from all precincts that were sampled. In multistage sampling, a researcher could introduce stratification. For instance, a researcher could first stratify the counties into rural, suburban, and urban and then separately draw counties at random from these three types of counties, thereby ensuring that all three types of counties are included in the sample.

Multistage random sampling is used in large-scale studies.

A technique that is sometimes useful is *random cluster sampling*. To use random cluster sampling, all members of a population must belong to a cluster (i.e., an existing group). For example, all Boy Scouts belong to troops; in most high schools, all students belong to homerooms; etc. Unlike simple random sampling in which individuals are drawn, in cluster sampling, *clusters* are drawn. To conduct a survey of Boy Scouts, for instance, a researcher could draw a random sample of troops, contact the leaders of the selected troops, and ask them to administer the questionnaires to all members of their troops.

In *random cluster sampling*, existing groups of participants are drawn.

There are two advantages of random cluster sampling over the other two types of random sampling discussed above. First, there are fewer individuals for a researcher to contact (e.g., only the troops' leaders and not the individual scouts). Second, the degree of cooperation is likely to be greater if troop leaders ask the individual scouts to participate than if a researcher who is unknown to the scouts asks them.

There is a disadvantage to random cluster sampling. For statistical reasons that are beyond the scope of this book, the number of clusters (not the number of participants) should be treated as the sample size. Thus, for instance, if 20 troops with 10 Boy Scouts each were selected, responses from 200 Boy Scouts would be obtained. However, the researcher would need to report the sample size as 20, not as 200. As a result, when using cluster sampling, it is desirable to use a large number of clusters to overcome the disadvantage.

As you know from Section 3, random sampling creates *sampling errors*. The inferential statistics described in this part of the book are designed to assess the impact of these errors on the results researchers obtain when they use random samples.

Endnotes

[1] This part of the book (Part D) describes *inferential statistics*, which are statistics that help assess the appropriateness of making *inferences* from a sample to a population.

[2] Examples of biased samples are provided in Section 3 of this book.

[3] Academic libraries have books of random numbers. Statistical computer programs can also generate them.

[4] The number of digits in the number names must equal the number of digits in the population total. For instance, if there are 500 people in a population, there are 3 digits in the total, and there must be 3 digits in each number name. Thus, the first case in the population is named 001, the second one is named 002, and so on.

[5] If your purpose was to compare men with women, then it would be acceptable to draw the same number of each and compare averages or percentages for the two samples.

[6] Of course, if your hunch that men and women differ in their opinion was wrong, the use of stratification would be of no benefit.

Exercise for Section 17

Note: If any of your answers include the term *random sampling*, indicate whether it is *simple, stratified, cluster,* or *multistage*.

Factual Questions

1. The most important characteristic of a good sample is that it is free from what?

2. If you put the names of all members of a population on slips of paper, mix them, and draw some, what type of sampling are you using?

3. If there are 60 members of a population and you give them all number names starting with 01, what are the number names of the *first two participants selected* if you select a sample starting at the beginning of the third row of the Table of Random Numbers in Appendix C near the end of this book?

4. If there are 500 members of a population and you give them all number names starting with 001, what are the number names of the *first two participants selected* if you select a sample starting at the beginning of the fourth row of the Table of Random Numbers in Appendix C near the end of this book?

5. In what type of sampling is the population first divided into strata that are believed to be relevant to the variable(s) being studied?

6. Suppose you draw at random the names of 5% of the registered voters separately from each county in a state. What type of sampling are you using?

7. Does stratification eliminate all sampling errors?

8. Suppose you draw a sample of 12 of the homerooms in a school district at random and administer a questionnaire to all students in the selected homerooms. What type of sampling are you using?

9. Suppose you draw a random sample of 20 hospitals from the population of hospitals in the United States, then draw a random sample of maternity wards from the 20 hospitals, and then draw a random sample of patients in the maternity wards previously selected. What type of sampling are you using?

Question for Discussion

10. Suppose you want to conduct a survey of a sample of the students registered at your college or university. Briefly describe how you would select the sample.

Notes:

Section 18

Sample Size

In Sections 3 and 17, you learned the importance of using random samples whenever possible. By using a random sampling, researchers draw unbiased samples. However, an unbiased random sample still contains random *sampling errors*. In other words, by the luck of the random draw, a random sample may differ from a population in important aspects. Fortunately, sampling errors can be evaluated with inferential statistics, which is the topic of the remaining sections in this part of the book. It is important to note, however, that inferential statistics cannot be used to evaluate the role of bias, which is why it is important to eliminate bias in the first place by using random sampling.

As a general rule, the larger the random sample, the smaller the sampling errors. In technical terms, the larger the random sample is, the more *precise* the results are. Statisticians define *precision* as the extent to which the same results would be obtained if another random sample were drawn from the same population. The basic way to increase precision is to increase sample size.[1] For instance, if a researcher drew two random samples of 500 individuals from a population, the two sets of results (e.g., the means for each sample of 500) would probably be closer than if the researcher had drawn two random samples of only 25 individuals each. Thus, a sample of 500 would be expected to have greater precision than a sample of 25.

While it is rather obvious that increasing sample size increases precision, it is less obvious that increasing sample size produces *diminishing returns* in terms of increasing precision. To understand diminishing returns, consider Examples 1 and 2 on the next page. In both examples, the researchers have added 10 individuals to their samples. Which researcher gets a bigger increase in precision by increasing the sample size by 10? The answer is Researcher A in Example 1. This researcher has doubled the sample size from 10 to 20 (a 100% increase), while Researcher B in Example 2 has increased his or her sample by only 1% (from 1,000 to 1,010).

An unbiased random sample contains *sampling errors.*

The larger the sample, the smaller the sampling errors and the greater the *precision.*

Increasing sample size produces *diminishing returns.*

95

Example 1:

Researcher A plans to sample 10 individuals at random from a large population. At the last minute, the researcher decides to increase precision by increasing the sample size to 20 by selecting 10 additional individuals for the sample.

Example 2:

Researcher B plans to sample 1,000 individuals at random from a large population. At the last minute, the researcher decides to increase precision by increasing the sample size to 1,010 by selecting 10 additional individuals for the sample.

Looking at Examples 1 and 2 from another perspective, we can see that the results obtained by the researcher in Example 1 could get a substantial change in results by increasing the sample size from 10 to 20. In contrast, the researcher in Example 2 can expect little effect on the results by adding 10 to a sample of 1,000.

Because of the principle of diminishing returns, even when researchers are conducting national opinion polls, samples of about 1,500 are usually quite adequate. Typically, adding more individuals to a sample of this size produces very little increase in the precision of results.[2]

Researchers often explore differences among groups of individuals. A general principle in determining sample size for examining group differences is this: *The smaller the anticipated difference in the population, the larger the sample size should be.* For instance, suppose a new drug has been developed for relieving headaches, and the pharmaceutical researchers anticipate that the new drug will be only slightly more effective than existing drugs. With very small samples (one sample taking the new drug and one sample taking existing drugs), researchers may not be able to detect the small difference because the results will be imprecise due to the limited sample size.

A corollary is this: *Even small samples can identify very large differences.* Suppose a researcher is testing a new antiviral treatment for a new strain of virus. The researcher uses random samples of 100 for the experimental group and 100 for the control group. (All individuals in both groups recently became ill with the virus.) Suppose,

For national opinion polls, samples of about 1,500 are usually adequate.

The smaller the anticipated difference in the population, the larger the sample size should be.

Even small samples can identify very large differences.

further, that of those who received the new treatment (the experimental group) only five died (5%), while of those who did not receive the new treatment, 45 died (45%). Because of the large size of the difference, this should be regarded as a very promising result even though the researcher studied a total of only 200 individuals. To put this into perspective, consider this practical question: If you became ill with the virus, would you take the new treatment even though there were only 100 in the treatment group (a small sample for this type of study) *or* would you reject the treatment and wait until the result was later replicated in studies with larger samples? If you would decide to take the treatment, you would be acknowledging the importance of the large difference obtained with the two relatively small samples.

When researchers determine sample size for their studies, they should also consider the variation in the population because of this principle: *For populations with very limited variability, even small samples can yield precise results.* For instance, if you take a random sample of eggs that have already been graded as "extra large" and weigh each egg, you will probably find only a small amount of variation among them. For this population, a small random sample should yield a precise estimate of the average weight of "extra large" eggs. The principle is made clearer by considering the highly hypothetical situation in Example 3. What size sample should the anthropologist in Example 3 use? Because there is essentially no variation in heights among identical twins that were raised identically, a sample size of 1 (one tribe member) should yield a highly precise answer.

> *For populations with very limited variability, even small samples can yield precise results.*

Example 3:

A anthropologist discovers a lost tribe that consists of 1,000 identical twins. They are not only genetically identical, they were all raised in the same way, ate the same diets, and so on. The anthropologist wants to estimate the average heights of the members of the tribe by using a sample.

A corollary is this: *The more variable the population, the larger the sample size should be.* For instance, suppose you wanted to estimate the math achievement of sixth-graders in a very large metropolitan school district and drew a random sample of only 30 students. Because there is likely to be tremendous variation in math ability

> *The more variable the population, the larger the sample size should be.*

across a large school district, a sample of 30, even though it is random, might yield very misleading results because of the lack of precision. By chance, for instance, you might obtain a disproportionately large number of high achievers. Using a much larger sample would greatly increase precision and thus reduce such a possibility.

Another principle in determining sample size is this: *When studying a rare phenomenon, large samples are usually required.* For example, suppose you wanted to estimate the percentage of college students who are HIV-positive. If you draw a sample of only about 100, you probably would find no cases because the disease is relatively rare and is unlikely to be evident in such a small sample; thus, you might mistakenly conclude that no college students are HIV-positive. By using a sample of thousands, you could get a precise estimate of the small percentage who are positive.

When studying a rare phenomenon, large samples are usually required.

The most important principle to remember when considering sample size is this: *Using a large sample does not correct for a bias.* For instance, if you are homeless and ask hundreds of your homeless friends how they feel about the government giving a $5,000 grant to each homeless individual, you may misjudge the opinions of the general public, which is your population. Even if you traveled around the country and asked thousands of homeless people you encountered about this issue, you probably would be just as much in error as you would be with a smaller, biased sample of just your homeless friends. This example illustrates that, in general, it is better to use a small, unbiased sample than a large, biased sample. Using a random process to select participants eliminates bias.

Using a large sample does not correct for a bias.

Concluding Comment

As you can see from the discussion above, determining sample size is a complex process. Thus, there is no simple answer to the question of how large a sample should be. As you work through the remainder of this book, sample size will be discussed again in various contexts because sample size affects the results obtained with inferential statistics, which is the topic of the remaining sections of this part of the book.

Endnotes

[1] Another way to increase precision is to use stratification. See the previous section of this book for a discussion of stratified random sampling.

[2] This is especially true when stratified random sampling is used (as it usually is in national samples) because stratification increases the precision of results over results obtained with simple random sampling.

Exercise for Section 18

Factual Questions

1. How do statisticians define the term *precision*?

2. What is the basic way to increase precision?

3. Suppose that Researcher Doe increased her sample size from 100 to 120, while Researcher Smith increased his sample size from 500 to 520. Which researcher will get a greater increase in precision by increasing the sample size by 20?

4. "The smaller the difference in the population, the larger the sample size should be." Is this statement "true" *or* "false"?

5. "Only very large samples can identify very large group differences." Is this statement "true" *or* "false"?

6. Suppose a researcher was planning to conduct a study on attitudes on a controversial topic and expects a wide degree of variation. Given that a wide degree of variation is expected, should the researcher use a "relatively large sample" *or* "a relatively small sample"?

7. "For populations with very limited variability, only very large samples can yield precise results." Is this statement "true" *or* "false"?

8. When studying the incidence of rare phenomena, should researchers use "relatively large samples" *or* use "relatively small samples"?

9. Does using a large sample correct for a bias?

Question for Discussion

10. Think about reports of research in the popular media such as TV newscasts. In your opinion, how important is it for the reports to include mention of the sample sizes? Explain.

Section 19

Standard Error of the Mean

Suppose there is a large population with a mean of 80 on a standardized test. Furthermore, suppose that a researcher does not have this information but wants to estimate the mean of the population by testing only a sample. When the researcher draws a *random sample* and administers the test to just the sample, will he or she correctly estimate the population mean as exactly 80? In all likelihood, the answer is "no" because random sampling introduces chance errors—known as *sampling errors*. These errors can affect the results.

At first, the situation may seem rather hopeless. Although bias has been eliminated by using random sampling, sampling errors created by the random selection process may still affect the results. Fortunately, however, random sampling errors have an effect on results that is predictable *in the long run*.

To understand the effects of random sampling error on results in the long run, consider a researcher who drew not just one random sample but many such samples from the population that has a mean of 80. Specifically, the researcher (1) drew a random sample of 60 from a population, tested the participants, and computed the mean for the sample; (2) then drew another random sample of 60 from the same population, tested the participants, and computed the mean for the second sample; (3) then drew a third random sample of 60 from the same population, tested the participants, and computed the mean for the third sample; and (4) continued drawing samples of 60, testing, and computing means an unlimited number of times. In all likelihood, each of these samples would yield somewhat different results because of the effects of random sampling error. Consider these hypothetical results for the first four random samples drawn by the researcher:

Sample 1: Mean = 70

Sample 2: Mean = 75

Sample 3: Mean = 85

Sample 4: Mean = 90

First, note that none of the results are correct (i.e., none of the samples have a mean of 80). Second, some of the results are too low (below 80), while some are too high (above 80). Most important, note that the average of all four sample means is, in fact, the population mean (i.e., $70 + 75 + 85 + 90 = 320/4 = 80$).[1]

The hypothetical researcher would then have a very large number of means (70, 75, 85, 90, and an indefinite number of others), which would create what is known as the *sampling distribution of means*. The *central limit theorem* says that the sampling distribution of means is normal in shape (i.e., forms the normal curve; see Section 7 to review this concept). The standard deviation of the sampling distribution is known as the *standard error of the mean* (SE_M), which as you will see below is a very useful statistic.

Of course, in practice, a researcher usually draws a single sample, tests it, and calculates its mean. Therefore, the researcher is not certain of the value of the population mean nor does he or she know the value of the standard error of the mean that would have been obtained if he or she had sampled repeatedly an indefinite number of times. Fortunately, researchers do know two very useful things:

1. The larger the sample, the smaller the standard error of the mean. This is because larger samples have greater precision.[2]

2. The less the variability in a population, the smaller the standard error of the mean because sampling from less variable populations yields more precise results.[3]

Given these two facts and some statistical theory not covered here, statisticians have developed a formula for estimating the standard error of the mean (SE_M) based on only the information a researcher has about a single random sample drawn from a population at random.[4] Example 1 shows how the standard error of the mean is sometimes reported after it has been calculated for a set of data.

Example 1:

"For the West Coast sample, $m = 75.00$, $s = 16.00$, $n = 64$, and $SE_M = 2.00$."

The SE_M in Example 1 is what statisticians call a *margin of error*, which should be used when interpreting the sample mean of 75.00.

According to the *central limit theorem*, the *sampling distribution of means* is normal.

The standard deviation of the *sampling distribution* is known as the *standard error of the mean* (SE_M).

The larger the sample, the smaller the standard error of the mean.

The less the variability in a population, the smaller the standard error of the mean.

The *standard error of the mean* is a *margin of error*.

As it turns out, the *standard error of the mean* is a type of standard deviation.[5] As you may recall from your study of the standard deviation earlier in this book, about 68% of the cases in a distribution lie within one standard deviation unit of the mean. Thus, because the standard error of the mean in Example 1 on the previous page equals 2.00 points, we would expect about 68% of all sample means to lie within 2.00 points of the true population mean.

About 68% of all sample means lie within one standard error of the mean.

Now, consider a practical use of the standard error of the mean. Specifically, it can be used to build a *68% confidence interval for a mean*. To calculate it based on the information in Example 1, simply subtract the SE_M from the mean ($75 - 2 = $ **73**) and add it to the mean ($75.00 + 2.00 = $ **77**). These two values (73 and 77) are the *limits of the 68% confidence interval for the mean*. In everyday terms, we can say that while the researcher obtained a mean of 75, its value might have been influenced by sampling errors. To account for these errors, a more reliable estimate of the true population mean is that it is between 73 and 77. We can say this with 68% confidence in the correctness of this statement.

By adding SE_M to the mean and subtracting SE_M from the mean, the *limits of the 68% confidence interval for the mean* are obtained.

When a researcher reports a single value (such as 75.00) as an estimate of a population mean based on a sample, it is called a *point estimate* of the mean. When a researcher reports the limits of a confidence interval (such as 73.00 to 77.00), it is called an *interval estimate* of the mean. It is usually desirable to report both a point estimate and an interval estimate (or at least report the point estimate as well as the associated standard error of the mean so that a consumer of research can calculate an interval estimate).

It is more common for researchers to report 95% or 99% confidence intervals instead of 68% intervals.[6] When there are several groups, the intervals are often reported in a table such as the one shown in Example 2.

95% and 99% confidence intervals are commonly reported.

Example 2:

Table 19.1

Selected Statistics for Two Groups of Participants

	n	m	s	95% C.I.
Group A	128	75.00	16.00	72.23 – 77.77
Group B	200	75.00	10.00	73.61 – 76.39

The 95% confidence intervals in Example 2 on the previous page indicate the range of score values in which we can have 95% confidence that the true (i.e., population) mean lies. Consider Group A. We can have 95% confidence that the true mean lies between 72.23 and 77.77.[7] Notice that we are still not absolutely certain of the value of the true population mean because the 128 participants are just a random sample of a population. However, we have a result (the 95% confidence interval) in which we can have a great deal of confidence as an accurate estimate of the population mean.

> A 95% confidence interval indicates the range of values in which we can have 95% confidence that the true mean lies.

It should be obvious that small confidence intervals are desirable. As it turns out, the size of the sample is an important factor in the computation of the standard error of the mean. By using reasonably large samples, researchers can minimize the size of the standard error of the mean and thereby obtain confidence intervals that are reasonably small.

> Using large samples keeps the standard error of the mean and confidence intervals small.

It is important to keep in mind that confidence intervals are valid only when the means are obtained with random sampling. If there is a bias creating errors, there are no general techniques for estimating the amount of error created by the bias nor is it possible to calculate meaningful confidence intervals. This illustrates the importance of using random samples whenever possible.

> Confidence intervals assist in interpreting means that are subject to random errors; they cannot take bias into account.

Endnotes

[1] While this example has only four sample means, it illustrates what would happen in the long run. In the long run, with an indefinitely large number of samples, the mean of the sample means obtained by random sampling will equal the true mean of the population. This is not true with biased sampling because a particular bias tends to push all the results off in one direction or the other.

[2] See Section 18 to review the relationship between sample size and precision.

[3] See Section 18 to review the relationship between variability and precision.

[4] The central limit theorem makes it possible to estimate the standard error of the mean given only one mean and the associated standard deviation.

[5] In fact, it is an estimate of the standard deviation of the sampling distribution of means.

[6] The formulas for building 95% and 99% confidence intervals are beyond the scope of this book.

[7] Technically, if a researcher drew 100 samples of 128 participants and constructed 95% confidence intervals for all 100 samples, about 95 of the 100 confidence intervals would include the true mean.

Exercise for Section 19

Factual Questions

1. "If bias has been eliminated, it is safe to assume that the sample is free of sampling errors." Is this statement "true" *or* "false"?

2. Are the effects of random sampling errors predictable in the long run?

3. If a researcher drew several random samples from a given population and measured the same trait for each sample, should he or she expect to obtain identical results each time?

4. "The larger the sample, the larger the standard error of the mean." Is this statement "true" *or* "false"?

5. Suppose a researcher found that $M = 30.00$ and $SE_M = 3.00$. What are the limits of the 68% confidence interval for the mean?

6. Suppose a researcher reported the mean and standard error of the mean. How should you calculate the limits of the 68% confidence interval for the mean?

7. What is the name of the type of estimate being reported when a researcher reports a single value as an estimate of a population mean based on a sample?

8. "It is more common to report the 68% confidence interval than to report the 95% or 99% confidence intervals." Is this statement "true" *or* "false"?

9. How can researchers minimize the size of the standard error of the mean?

Question for Discussion

10. Suppose that you read that the mean for a sample equals 100.00 and the limits of the 95% C.I. are 95.00 and 105.00. Briefly explain what the limits tell you.

Notes:

Section 20

Introduction to the Null Hypothesis

Suppose a researcher selected a random sample of first-grade girls and a random sample of first-grade boys from a large school district in order to estimate the average reading achievement of each sample on a standardized test. Further, suppose the researcher obtained these means:

Girls	Boys
$m = 50.00$	$m = 46.00$

This result suggests that girls, on the average, have higher achievement in reading than boys. But do they really? Remember that the researcher tested only random samples of the boys and the girls. Thus, it is possible that the difference the researcher obtained is due only to the errors created by random sampling, which are known as *sampling errors*. In other words, it is possible that the population mean for boys and the population mean for girls are identical, and that the researcher found a difference between the means of the two randomly selected samples only because of the chance errors associated with random sampling. This possibility is known as the *null hypothesis*. For the difference between two sample means, it says that:

The true difference between the means (in the population) is zero.

This statement can also be expressed with symbols, as follows:[1]

$H_0: \mu_1 - \mu_2 = 0$

Where:

H_0 is the symbol for the null hypothesis.

μ_1 is the symbol for the *population* mean for one group (such as all boys).

μ_2 is the symbol for the *population* mean for the other group (such as all girls).

The difference between two means may be due only to *sampling errors.*

For two sample means, the *null hypothesis* says that the true difference between the means is zero.

In everyday language, the symbols above state that the difference between the means of two populations equals zero. Thus, another way to state the null hypothesis is:

There is no true difference between the means.

The null hypothesis may also be stated in the positive (without the word "no") as follows:

The observed difference between the sample means was created by sampling error.

Most researchers are interested in identifying differences among groups and are typically seeking explanations for the differences that they find. Therefore, most researchers do not undertake their studies in the hope of confirming the null hypothesis. In other words, they usually expect differences (i.e., they hypothesize that differences exist).

A researcher's "expectation" is called a *research hypothesis*. For instance, a researcher might have a research hypothesis that the average reading achievement of girls is higher than that of boys. Because the research hypothesis states that one particular group's average is higher than the other group's, this research hypothesis is known as a *directional research hypothesis*. Expressed as symbols, this hypothesis is:

$H_1: \mu_1 > \mu_2$

Where:

H_1 is the symbol for an *alternative hypothesis* (i.e., an alternative to the null hypothesis), which in this case is a *directional research hypothesis*.

μ_1 is the symbol for the population mean for the group hypothesized to have a higher mean (in this case, the girls).

μ_2 is the symbol for the population mean for the other group (in this case, the boys).

The symbols directly above indicate that a researcher has a hypothesis (H_1) that states that the population mean for one group (μ_1) is greater than (>) the population mean for the other group (μ_2).

Another researcher may hold a *nondirectional research hypothesis* as his or her *research hypothesis*. That is, the researcher

There are alternative ways to express the null hypothesis.

A researcher's personal hypothesis is known as the research hypothesis.

A directional research hypothesis states that one group is higher than the other.

A nondirectional research hypothesis is also a possibility.

might hypothesize that there is a difference between boys' and girls' reading achievement but that there is insufficient information to hypothesize which group is higher. In other words, the researcher is hypothesizing that there is a difference (that the populations of the two groups are not equal) but he or she is not willing to speculate on the direction of the difference. This is how to state a nondirectional research hypothesis in symbols:

H_1: $\mu_1 \neq \mu_2$

Where:

H_1 is the symbol for an *alternative hypothesis* (i.e., an alternative to the null hypothesis), which in this case is a *nondirectional research hypothesis*.

μ_1 is the symbol for the population mean for one group.

μ_2 is the symbol for the population mean for the other group.

The symbols immediately above indicate that a researcher has a hypothesis (H_1) that states that the mean for one population (μ_1) is not equal to ($\neq$) the mean for the other population (μ_2).

Suppose that the two means we considered at the beginning of this section (i.e., $m = 50.00$ for girls and $m = 46.00$ for boys) were obtained by a researcher who started with the directional research hypothesis that girls achieve a higher mean in reading than boys. Clearly, the observed means support the research hypothesis, but is the researcher finished? Obviously not because two possible explanations for the observed difference remain:

1. Girls have higher achievement in reading than boys. (This is the research hypothesis.)

2. The observed difference between the samples is solely the result of the effects of random sampling errors. Therefore, there is no true difference. (This is the null hypothesis.)

The *null hypothesis* is a possible explanation for an observed difference when there are *sampling errors*.

If the researcher stops at this point, he or she has two explanations for a single difference of four points between the mean of 50.00 for girls and the mean of 46.00 for boys. This is hardly a definitive result. As it turns out, the branch of statistics known as *inferential statistics* has statistical techniques (known as *inferential tests*) that can be used to test the truth of the null hypothesis. If an inferential test allows a researcher to eliminate the null hypothesis, then only the research hypothesis remains, and the researcher can appropriately assert that the data support the research hypothesis.

Note that all researchers who sample need to address the issue of the null hypothesis. Like it or not, when only random samples have been studied, researchers may be observing differences that are only the result of sampling errors. Thus, the null hypothesis is a possible explanation for any observed difference based on random samples.

Section 21 provides more about the null hypothesis, and the remaining sections of this book describe specific inferential tests of the null hypothesis.

Endnote

[1] See Appendix D near the end of this book for other ways to express the null hypothesis.

Exercise for Section 20

Factual Questions

1. What is the name of the hypothesis that states that a researcher has found a difference between the means of the two randomly selected samples only because of the chance errors associated with random sampling?

2. A researcher's "expectation" is called what?

3. If a researcher believes that Group A will have a higher mean than Group B, is his or her research hypothesis "directional" *or* "nondirectional"?

4. Consider this hypothesis, which is expressed in symbols: $H_1: \mu_1 > \mu_2$. Is this a "directional" *or* "nondirectional" hypothesis?

5. What is the symbol for the null hypothesis?

6. What is the symbol for an alternative hypothesis?

7. For what does the symbol μ_1 stand?

8. What is the name of the branch of statistics that has statistical techniques that can be used to test the truth of the null hypothesis?

Question for Discussion

9. A researcher has studied *all* the girls and *all* the boys in the populations of boys and girls in a school. The researcher has found a difference between the mean for boys and the mean for girls. Is the null hypothesis a possible explanation for the difference? Explain.

Notes:

Section 21

Decisions About the Null Hypothesis

As you know from the previous section, the null hypothesis states that there is no true difference between two sample means (i.e., in the population, the difference is zero). In other words, it asserts that an *observed difference*[1] between means was obtained only because of sampling errors created by random sampling errors. The remaining sections of this book deal with *tests of the null hypothesis*, which are commonly called *significance tests*.

As its final result, a significance test yields a *probability that the null hypothesis is true*. The symbol for probability is an italicized, lowercase *p*. Thus, if a researcher finds in a given study that the probability that the null hypothesis is true is a probability of less than 5 in 100, this result would be expressed as "$p < .05$." How should this be interpreted? What does it indicate about the null hypothesis? Quite simply, it indicates that it is *unlikely* that the null hypothesis is true. If it is unlikely to be true, what should we conclude about it? We should conclude that it is probably not true.

It is important to understand how to interpret values of *p*, so consider an analogy that makes it clearer. Suppose a weather reporter states that the probability of rain tomorrow is less than 5 in 100. What should we conclude? First, we know that there is some chance of rain—but it is very small. Because of its low probability, most people would conclude that it probably will not rain and not make any special preparations for rain. For all practical purposes, they have rejected the hypothesis that it will rain tomorrow. Likewise, when there is a low probability that the null hypothesis is correct, researchers reject the null hypothesis.

There is always some probability that the null hypothesis is true, so if a researcher waits for certainty, he or she will never be able to make a decision. Thus, applied researchers have settled on the .05 level as the most conventional level at which it is appropriate to make a decision (i.e., decide to reject the null hypothesis, which is done when the probability is .05 or less).[2]

An inferential test of a null hypothesis yields a *probability* (*p*) *that the null hypothesis is true.*

When *p* is less than 5 in 100 that something is true, it is conventional to regard it as *unlikely* to be true.

When researchers use the .05 level, they are, in effect, willing to be wrong 5 times in 100 when rejecting the null hypotheses. Consider the rain analogy above. If we make no special preparations for rain 100 days for which the probability of rain is .05, it will probably rain 5 of those 100 days. Thus, in rejecting the null hypothesis, we are taking a calculated risk that we might be wrong. This type of error is known as a *Type I Error*—the error of rejecting the null hypothesis when it is correct. On those 5 days in 100 when you are caught in the rain without your rain gear, you will get wet because you made 5 Type I Errors.

> A *Type I Error* is the error of rejecting the null hypothesis when it is correct.

A synonym for "rejecting the null hypothesis" is "declaring a result to be statistically significant." In academic journals, statements such as this one are common: *The difference between the means is statistically significant at the .05 level.* This statement indicates that the researcher has rejected the null hypothesis because the probability of its truth is 5 or less in 100.

> A synonym for *rejecting the null hypothesis* is declaring a result to be *statistically significant.*

In journals, you will frequently find *p* values of less than .05 reported. The most common are $p < .01$ (less than 1 in 100) and $p < .001$ (less than 1 in 1,000). When a result is statistically significant at these levels, investigators can be more confident that they are making the right decision in rejecting the null hypothesis than when they use the .05 level. Clearly, if there is only 1 chance in 100 that something is true, it is less likely that it is true than if there are 5 chances in 100 that it is true. For this reason, the .01 level is a *higher* level of significance than the .05 level, and the .001 level is a *higher* level of significance than the .01 level. They are called *higher levels* because at the .01 and .001 levels, the odds are *greater* that the null hypothesis is correctly being rejected than at the .05 level.

> The lower the probability, the higher the level of significance. For example, $p < .01$ is a *higher* level of significance than $p < .05$.

In review:

.06+ level: *not* significant, do *not* reject the null hypothesis.

.05 level: significant, reject the null hypothesis.

.01 level: more significant, reject the null hypothesis with more confidence than at the .05 level.

.001 level: highly significant, reject the null hypothesis with more confidence than at the .01 or .05 levels.

So what probability level should be used? Remember that most researchers are looking for significant differences (or relationships). Thus, they are most likely to use the .05 level because this is the easiest to achieve.[3]

In inferential statistics, a probability (*p*) refers to the probability of making a Type I Error. It is also possible to make a *Type II Error*, which is the error of failing to reject the null hypothesis when it is false. To understand the difference between Type I and Type II Errors, consider Examples 1 and 2.

A *Type II Error* is the error of failing to reject the null hypothesis when it is false.

Example 1: An example of a Type I Error.

The mean self-concept in a population of girls is 50, and the mean self-concept in a population of boys is 50. Thus, the two populations are, on average, equal. A researcher draws a random sample of girls and a random sample of boys and observes a mean of 52 for girls and a mean of 48 for boys. An inferential statistical test indicates that *p is less than .05* (*p < .05*), so the researcher rejects the null hypothesis. The researcher has unknowingly made a Type I Error because he or she has rejected the null hypothesis, which *correctly* states that there is no difference between the population means.

Example 2: An example of a Type II Error.

The mean arithmetic reasoning test score in a population of girls is 20, and the mean in a population of boys is 18. Thus, the two populations are, on average, *not* equal. A researcher draws a random sample of girls and a random sample of boys and observes a mean of 21 for girls and a mean of 19 for boys. An inferential statistical test indicates that *p is greater than .05* (*p > .05*), so the researcher does *not* reject the null hypothesis. The researcher has unknowingly made a Type II Error because he or she has *not* rejected the null hypothesis, which *incorrectly* states that there is no difference between the population means.

Carefully considering Examples 1 and 2 will help in understanding the difference between the two types of errors. It is important to note that in both examples the researcher does *not* know the population means, nor does he or she know that an error has been made by making decisions based on values of *p*.

In review, there are two types of errors that may be made when making a decision about the null hypothesis:

Type I Error: Reject the null hypothesis when, in reality, it is true.

Type II Error: Fail to reject the null hypothesis when, in reality, it is false.

At first, this might seem frustrating—researchers have done their best, but are still faced with the possibility of making two types of errors. Nevertheless, by using probabilities, researchers make informed decisions in the face of uncertainty. Either decision about the null hypothesis (reject *or* fail to reject) may be wrong, but by using inferential statistics to make the decisions, researchers are making calculated decisions that are consistent with the probabilities.

Because the decision on rejecting the null hypothesis can be wrong in any given case, it is important to examine groups of studies when making generalizations about what is true on any given topic. Across a group of studies on a topic, isolated errors regarding the null hypothesis will be washed out by the majority of other studies. Using probabilities in the way described here makes it very likely that the majority of studies on a given topic are correct in either rejecting or not rejecting the null hypothesis.

In this section and the previous section, the emphasis has been on using probabilities in comparing means because this is one of the most common uses for inferential statistics. The following four sections provide more information on statistical tests of significance for means. In addition, frequencies are often compared. This type of comparison is discussed in Section 26 of this book.[4]

> Researchers make informed decisions using probabilities in the face of uncertainty.

Endnotes

[1]An "observed difference" is the difference a researcher obtains. It may not represent a true difference because of the influence of random sampling errors.

[2]The probability level for rejecting the null hypothesis is known as the *alpha level*.

[3]However, if they find that their result is significant at the .01 or .001 levels, they will usually report it at these levels for the readers' information.

[4]All other descriptive statistics may be compared for significance using inferential statistical tests. For instance, there are tests for comparing medians, standard deviations, and correlation coefficients. Although the mathematical procedures are different, in any such comparison there is a null hypothesis that attributes

differences to sampling errors. Decisions about the null hypotheses for these and other descriptive statistics are made using the same probability levels discussed in this section.

Exercise for Section 21

Factual Questions

1. What does an inferential test of a null hypothesis yield as its final result?

2. Which of the following indicates that the probability is less than 5 in 100? (Circle one.)

   A. $p < .05$.   B. $p > .05$.

3. What is a synonym for the phrase "rejecting the null hypothesis"?

4. What is the name of the error of rejecting the null hypothesis when it is true?

5. If a difference is declared to be statistically significant, what decision is being made about the null hypothesis?

6. Is the ".05 level" *or* the ".01 level" more significant?

7. Is the ".01 level" *or* the ".001 level" more significant?

8. When $p < .05$, is the difference usually regarded as "statistically significant" *or* "statistically insignificant"?

9. When $p > .05$, is the difference usually regarded as "statistically significant" *or* "statistically insignificant"?

10. Is it possible for a researcher to reject the null hypothesis with absolute certainty?

Notes:

Section 22

Introduction to the *t* Test

Researchers frequently need to determine the statistical significance of the difference between two sample means. Consider Example 1, which illustrates the need for making such a comparison.

Example 1:

A researcher wanted to determine whether there are differences between men and women voters in their attitudes toward welfare. Separate samples of men and women were drawn at random and administered an attitude scale. Women had a mean of 38.00 (on a scale from 0 to 50, where 50 is the most favorable attitude). Men had a mean of 35.00. The researcher wants to determine whether there is a significant difference between the two means. What accounts for the 3-point difference between a mean of 38 and a mean of 35? One possible explanation is that the population of women has a more favorable attitude than the population of men, and that the two samples correctly reflect this difference between the two populations. Another possible explanation is raised by the *null hypothesis*, which states that there is no true difference between men and women—that the observed difference is due to sampling errors created by random sampling.

About a hundred years ago, a statistician named William Gosset developed the *t test* for exactly the situation described in Example 1 (i.e., to test the difference between two sample means to determine statistical significance).[1] As a test of the null hypothesis, the *t* test yields a probability that a given null hypothesis is correct. As indicated in Section 21, when there is a low probability that it is correct—say as low as .05 (5%) or less—researchers usually reject the null hypothesis.

The computational procedures for conducting *t* tests are beyond the scope of this book. However, the following material describes what makes the *t* test work. In other words, what leads the *t* test to yield a low probability that the null hypothesis is correct for a

This section deals with how to compare two sample means for statistical significance.

When the *t test* yields a low probability that a null hypothesis is correct, researchers usually reject the null hypothesis.

given pair of means? Here are the three basic factors, which interact with each other in determining the probability level:

1. The larger the samples, the less likely the difference between two means was created by sampling errors. This is because larger samples have less sampling error than smaller samples. Other things being equal, when large samples are used, the *t* test is more likely to yield a probability low enough to allow rejection of the null hypothesis than when small samples are used. Put another way: When there is less sampling error, there is less of a chance that the null hypothesis (an assertion that sampling error created the difference) is correct. In other words, when there is great precision because large samples are used, researchers can be more confident that their sample results reflect the underlying difference in a population than when small samples are used.

   The larger the sample, the more likely the null hypothesis will be rejected.

2. The larger the observed difference between the two means, the less likely that the difference was created by sampling errors. Random sampling tends to create many small differences and few large ones (especially if large samples are used). Thus, when large differences between means are obtained, the *t* test is more likely to yield a probability low enough to allow rejection of the null hypothesis than when small differences are obtained.

   The larger the observed difference between two means, the more likely the null hypothesis will be rejected.

3. The smaller the variance among the participants, the less likely it is that the difference between two means was created by sampling errors and the more likely the null hypothesis will be rejected. To understand this principle, consider a population in which there is no variance because everyone is identical: All members of the population look alike, think alike, as well as speak and act in unison. How many participants does a researcher have to sample from this population to get an accurate result? Obviously, only one participant because all members of the population are identical. Thus, when there is no variation among the members of a population, it is not possible to have sampling errors when sampling from the population. If there are no sampling errors, the null hypothesis should be rejected. As the variation increases, sampling errors are more and more likely to be the cause of an observed difference between means.[2]

   The smaller the variance, the more likely the null hypothesis will be rejected.

There are two types of *t* tests. One is for *independent data* (sometimes called *uncorrelated data*) and one is for *dependent data* (sometimes called *correlated data*). Example 1 on page 119 has independent data, which means that there is no pairing or matching of individuals across the two samples. The men and women were drawn independently from the two populations without regard to whether each individual in one group "matches" in any way (such as age) an individual in another group. The meaning of independent data becomes clearer when contrasted with dependent data, which is illustrated in Example 2.

Example 1 illustrates independent data.

Example 2:

In a study of visual acuity, pairs of same-sex siblings (two brothers or two sisters) were identified for a study. For each pair of siblings, a coin was tossed to determine which one received a vitamin supplement and which one received a placebo. Thus, for each participant in the experimental group, there was a same-sex sibling in the control group.

Example 2 illustrates dependent data.

The means that result from the study in Example 2 are less subject to sampling error than the means from Example 1 on page 119. Remember that in Example 1 there was no matching or pairing of participants before assignment to conditions. In Example 2, the matching of participants assures us that the two groups are more similar than if just any two independent samples were used. To the extent that genetics and gender are associated with visual acuity, the two groups in Example 2 will be more similar at the onset of the experiment than the two groups in Example 1. The *t* test for dependent data takes this possible reduction of error into account.[3] Researchers will often mention in their reports whether they conducted *t* tests for independent or for dependent data.

Dependent data may have less sampling error.

The next section illustrates how to interpret reports of *t* tests.

Endnotes

[1] As indicated in Section 21, when a result is statistically significant, the null hypothesis is rejected.

[2] In the types of studies we are considering, researchers do not know the variation in population. However, the *t* test uses the standard deviations of the samples to estimate the variation of the population. In other words, the standard deviations of the samples provide the *t* test with an indication of the amount of variation in the populations from which the samples were drawn.

[3] Ideally, we would like to conduct an experiment in which the two groups are initially *identical* in their visual acuity.

Exercise for Section 22

Factual Questions

1. Example 1 mentions how many possible explanations for the 3-point difference?

2. What is the name of the hypothesis that states that the observed difference is due to sampling errors created by random sampling?

3. Which of the following statements is true? (Circle one.)
   A. The *t* test is used to test the difference between two sample means to determine statistical significance.
   B. The *t* test is used to test the difference between two population means to determine statistical significance.

4. If a *t* test yields a low probability such as $p < .05$, what decision is usually made about the null hypothesis?

5. The larger the sample, the (circle one)
   A. more likely the null hypothesis will be rejected.
   B. less likely the null hypothesis will be rejected.

6. The smaller the observed difference between two means, the (circle one)
   A. more likely the null hypothesis will be rejected.
   B. less likely the null hypothesis will be rejected.

7. If there is no variation among members of a population, is it possible to have sampling errors when sampling from the population?

8. If participants are first paired before being randomly assigned to experimental and control groups, are the resulting data "independent" *or* "dependent"?

9. Which type of data tend to have less sampling error? (Circle one.)
   A. Independent.
   B. Dependent.

Section 23

Reports of the Results of *t* Tests

In Section 22, the use of the *t* test to test the difference between two sample means for significance was considered. Obviously, the values of the means should be reported before reporting the results of the statistical test performed on them. In addition, the values of the standard deviations and the number of cases in each group should be reported first. This may be done within the context of a sentence or in a table. Table 23.1 shows a typical table.

Table 23.1
Means and Standard Deviations

	m	*s*	*n*
Group A	2.50	1.87	6
Group B	6.00	1.89	6

The samples for Groups A and B were drawn at random. The null hypothesis states that the 3.50 point difference (6.00 − 2.50 = 3.50) between the means of 2.50 and 6.00 is the result of sampling errors (i.e., errors resulting from random sampling) and that the true difference in the population is zero.

The result of a significant *t* test may be described in several ways. Below are some examples for the results in Table 23.1 above. The statement in Example 1 implies that the null hypothesis has been rejected because the term *statistically significant* is synonymous with *rejecting the null hypothesis.*

Example 1:

The difference between the means is statistically significant ($t = 3.22$, $df = 10$, $p < .01$).

In Example 2 on the next page, the researcher has used slightly different wording to indicate that significance was obtained at the .01 level. The phrase *significant at the .01 level* indicates that *p* was equal to or less than .01. Thus, the null hypothesis was rejected.

Example 2:

The difference between the means is significant at the .01 level ($t = 3.22$, $df = 10$).

Example 3 below provides the same information as Example 1 and Example 2 but with different wording. The sentence indicates that the difference is statistically significant because *rejecting the null hypothesis* is the same as *declaring statistical significance.*

Example 3:

The null hypothesis was rejected at the .01 level ($t = 3.22$, $df = 10$).

Any of the forms of expression illustrated in the above three examples is acceptable. However, authors of journal articles seldom explicitly mention the null hypothesis. Instead, they tend to use the forms of expression in Examples 1 and 2. In theses and dissertations, in contrast, explicit references to the null hypothesis are more common.

When researchers use the word *significant* when reporting the results of significance tests, they should modify it with the adjective *statistically*. This is because a result may be *statistically significant* but may not be of any *practical significance*. For instance, suppose a researcher found a statistically significant difference of 2 points in favor of a computer-assisted approach over a traditional lecture/textbook approach. While it is statistically significant, it may not be of practical significance if the school district has to invest sizable amounts of money to buy new hardware and software. In other words, the cost of the difference may be too great in light of the absolute size of the benefit.[1]

Now, consider how researchers report the results of a *t* test when the difference between means is not statistically significant. Table 23.2 presents descriptive statistics. Examples 4 through 6 show some ways to express the results of the insignificant *t* test for the data in the table.

Rejecting the null hypothesis is the same as *declaring statistical significance.*

A result may be *statistically significant* but not be of any *practical significance.*

Table 23.2
Means and Standard Deviations

	m	*s*	*n*
Group A	8.14	2.19	7
Group B	5.71	2.81	7

The fact that *p* is *greater than* (>) .05 in Example 4 indicates that the null hypothesis was not rejected.

Example 4:

The difference between the means is not statistically significant ($t = 1.80$, $df = 12$, $p > .05$).

The author of Example 5 has used the abbreviation *n.s.* to indicate that the difference is *not significant*. Because the example does not indicate a specific probability level, most readers will assume that it was not significant at the .05 level—the most liberal of the widely used levels.[2] Example 4 is preferable to Example 5 because Example 4 indicates the specific probability level that was used to test the null hypothesis.

Example 5:

For the difference between the means, $t = 1.80$ ($df = 12$, *n.s.*).

Example 6 shows how the results of the test might be expressed with explicit reference to the null hypothesis.

Example 6:

The null hypothesis for the difference between the means was not rejected at the .05 level ($t = 1.80$, $df = 12$).

While reading journal articles, theses, and dissertations, you will find variations in the exact words used to describe the results of *t* tests. The examples in this section illustrate some of the most widely used forms of expression.

Examples 4, 5, and 6 show how the results of an insignificant *t* test may be reported.

The abbreviation *n.s.* means *not significant*.

It is best to indicate the specific probability level at which the null hypothesis was not rejected.

Endnotes

[1] Practical significance is considered again in Section 27.

[2] The .05 level is the "most liberal" in the sense that it is the level that is most likely to permit rejection of the null hypothesis. In other words, if a researcher uses the .01 or .001 levels, he or she is less likely to reject the null hypothesis than if the .05 level is used.

Exercise for Section 23

Factual Questions

1. Which statistics should be reported before reporting the results of a *t* test?

2. Suppose you read this statement: "The difference between the means is statistically significant at the .05 level ($t = 2.333$, $df = 11$)." Should you conclude that the null hypothesis has been rejected?

3. Suppose you read this statement: "The null hypothesis was rejected ($t = 2.810$, $df = 40$, $p < .01$)." Should you conclude that the difference is statistically significant?

4. Suppose you read this statement: "The null hypothesis was not rejected ($t = -.926$, $df = 24$, $p > .05$)." Describe in words the meaning of the statistical term "$p > .05$."

5. For the statement in Question 4, should you conclude that the difference is statistically significant?

6. Suppose you read this statement: "For the difference between the means, $t = 2.111$ ($df = 5$, *n.s.*)." Should you conclude that the null hypothesis has been rejected?

7. Which type of author seldom explicitly mentions the null hypothesis?

   A. Authors of dissertations.
   B. Authors of journal articles.

Section 24

One-Way ANOVA

The *t* test, which tests the null hypothesis regarding the difference between *two* means, was covered in Sections 22 and 23. A closely related statistical procedure is *analysis of variance (ANOVA)*, which performs what is called an *F* test. An *F* test can be used to test the difference(s) among *two or more* means.

Like the *t* test, ANOVA can be used to test the difference between two means. When this is done, the resulting *probability* will be the same as the probability that would have been obtained using a *t* test. However, the value of *F* will not be the same as the value of *t*.[1]

ANOVA can also be used to test the differences among more than two means in a single test, which cannot be done with a *t* test. Consider Example 1:

Example 1:

A new drug for treating migraine headaches was tested on three samples selected at random from a population. The first group received 250 milligrams, the second received 100 milligrams, and the third received a placebo (an inert substance). The average reported pain for the three groups (on a scale from 0 to 20, with 20 representing the most pain) was determined by calculating means. The means for the groups were:

Group 1: *M* = 1.78
Group 2: *M* = 3.98
Group 3: *M* = 12.88

As you can see in Example 1, there are three differences among means:

1. The difference between Groups 1 and 2 (1.78 versus 3.98).

2. The difference between Groups 1 and 3 (1.78 versus 12.88).

3. The difference between Groups 2 and 3 (3.98 versus 12.88).

Instead of running three separate *t* tests,[2] a researcher can run a single *F* test using ANOVA to test the significance of this *set of three*

ANOVA is used to test the difference(s) among two or more means.

The *set* of three differences in Example 1 can be tested with a single ANOVA.

differences. Examples 2 and 3 show two ways the results of an *F* test for Example 1 could be reported.

Example 2:

The difference among the means was statistically significant at the .01 level ($F = 58.769$, $df = 2, 36$).

Note that the statement in Example 2 is similar in structure to that for reporting the results of a *t* test (see Section 23). The statement indicates that there is a significant difference with $p < .01$. Thus, the null hypothesis may be rejected at the .01 level. The null hypothesis for this test says that the *set of three differences* was created at random. By rejecting the null hypothesis, a researcher is rejecting the notion that *one or more* of the differences were created at random by sampling error. Notice that the test does not indicate which of the three differences is responsible for the rejection of the null hypothesis but that *at least one of the three differences* is statistically significant.[3]

Example 3 shows a second way that the results of *F* tests conducted with ANOVA are commonly reported in journals. It is called an *ANOVA table*. The table shows the same values of *F*, *df*, and *p* that are reported in Example 2. The table also shows the values of the *sum of squares* and *mean square*, which are intermediate values obtained in the calculation of *F*. (For example, if you divide the mean square of 315.592 by the mean square of 5.370, you will obtain *F*.) For the typical consumer of research, the values of the sum of squares and mean square are of little interest. The typical consumer is primarily interested in whether the null hypothesis has been rejected, which is indicated by the value of *p*.

Example 3:

Table 1

Analysis of Variance Table for the Data in Example 1

Source of variation	*df*	Sum of squares	Mean square	*F*
Between groups	2	631.185	315.592	58.769[*]
Within groups	36	193.320	5.370	
Total	38	824.505		

[*]$p < .01$

> The method of reporting the results of an ANOVA is sometimes similar to the method for a *t* test.
>
> When a researcher rejects the null hypothesis, with ANOVA, the researcher is rejecting the notion that *one or more* of the differences in the set were created at random.
>
> An *ANOVA table* is sometimes used to report the results.
>
> The *sum of squares* and *mean square* in an ANOVA table are of little interest to the typical consumer of research.

Notice that the probability (*p*) in Example 3 on the previous page is given in a footnote, which is common in statistical reporting. Often, the value of *p* will be given in an ANOVA table as well as in the text of the research report. For instance, a researcher might include a statement like the one in Example 2 on the previous page in the text and refer the reader to a table such as the one in Example 3 on the previous page.

ANOVA can be used with a large number of means. Consider Example 4. A single ANOVA can determine whether the null hypothesis for the entire set of six differences should be rejected. If the result is not significant, the researcher is done. If the result is significant, he or she may conduct additional tests to determine which specific difference(s) is (are) significant.[4] While these additional tests are beyond the scope of this book, you will be able to understand them because they all result in a probability level (*p*), which is used to determine significance.

It is common to report the probability level in a footnote to an ANOVA table.

Example 4:

Four methods of teaching computer literacy were used in an experiment, which resulted in four means. This produced these six differences:

1. The difference between Methods 1 and 2.

2. The difference between Methods 1 and 3.

3. The difference between Methods 1 and 4.

4. The difference between Methods 2 and 3.

5. The difference between Methods 2 and 4.

6. The difference between Methods 3 and 4.

When there are four means, there are six differences among pairs of means.

The examples we have been considering are examples of what is known as a *one-way ANOVA* (also known as a *single-factor ANOVA*). This term is derived from the fact that participants were classified in only *one* way. In Example 1 on page 127, they were classified only according to the drug group to which they were assigned. In Example 4, they were classified only according to the method of instruction to which they were exposed.

In a one-way ANOVA, participants are classified in only one way.

Section 25 introduces and illustrates a *two-way ANOVA* (also known as a *two-factor ANOVA*) in which each participant is classified in two ways such as (1) which drug group they were assigned to and

(2) whether each participant is male or female. A two-way ANOVA permits researchers to answer interesting questions such as: Are some drugs more effective for treating men than they are for treating women?

Endnotes

[1] Historically, the *t* test preceeded ANOVA. Because ANOVA will also test the difference between two means, the *t* test is no longer needed. However, for instructional purposes, the *t* test is still taught in introductory statistics classes, and it is still widely used by researchers when only two means are being compared.

[2] It would be inappropriate to run three separate *t* tests without adjusting the probabilities for interpreting *t*. Such adjustments are not straightforward. However, a single *F* test automatically makes appropriate adjustments to the probabilities.

[3] Procedures for determining which individual differences are significant are beyond the scope of this book.

[4] A number of different tests, which do not always lead to the same conclusions, are available. Some that you may encounter are Tukey's *HSD* Test and Scheffé's Test.

Exercise for Section 24

Factual Questions

1. *ANOVA* stands for what three words?

2. What is the name of the test that can be conducted with an ANOVA?

3. "An ANOVA can be appropriately used to test *only* the difference between two means." Is this statement "true" *or* "false"?

4. If the difference between a pair of means is tested with ANOVA, will the probability level be different than if the difference was tested with a *t* test?

5. Which statistic in an ANOVA table is of the greatest interest to the typical consumer of research?

6. Suppose you read this statement: "The difference between the means was not statistically significant at the .05 level ($F = 2.293$, $df = 12, 18$)." Should you conclude that the null hypothesis was rejected?

7. Suppose you read this statement: "The difference between the means was statistically significant at the .01 level ($F = 3.409$, $df = 14, 17$)." Should you conclude that the null hypothesis was rejected?

8. Suppose you saw this in the footnote to a one-way ANOVA table: "$p < .05$." Are the differences statistically significant?

9. Suppose participants were classified according to their grade level in order to test the differences among the means for the grade levels. Does this call for a "one-way ANOVA" *or* a "two-way ANOVA"?

10. Suppose that the participants were classified according to their grade levels and their country of birth in order to study differences among means for both grade level and country of birth. Does this call for a "one-way ANOVA" *or* a "two-way ANOVA"?

Question for Discussion

11. Briefly describe a hypothetical study in which it would be appropriate to conduct a one-way ANOVA but would *not* be appropriate to conduct a *t* test.

Notes:

Section 25

Two-Way ANOVA

In a *two-way ANOVA* (also known as a *two-factor ANOVA*), participants are classified in two ways. Consider Example 1, which illustrates a two-way ANOVA.

In a *two-way ANOVA*, participants are classified in two ways.

Example 1:

A random sample of welfare recipients was assigned to a new job-training program. Another random sample was assigned to a conventional job-training program. (*Note*: The type of job-training program they were assigned to is one of the ways in which the participants were classified.) Participants were also classified according to whether or not they had a high school diploma. All of the participants in each group found employment in the private sector at the end of their training. Their mean hourly wages are shown in this table:[1]

	Type of program		
	Conventional	New	**Row means**
H.S. diploma	$M = \$8.88$	$M = \$8.75$	$M = \$8.82$
No H.S. diploma	$M = \$4.56$	$M = \$8.80$	$M = \$6.68$
Column means	$M = \$6.72$	$M = \$8.78$	

First, consider the column means of $6.72 (for the conventional program) and $8.78 (for the new program). These suggest that, overall, the new program is superior to the conventional one. In other words, if we temporarily ignore whether participants have a high school diploma, the new program seems superior to the conventional one. This difference ($8.78 − $6.72 = $2.06) suggests that there is what is called a *main effect*. A *main effect* is the result of comparing one of the ways in which the participants were classified while temporarily ignoring the other way in which they were classified.

Because the concept of a *main effect* can be difficult to grasp at first, consider it again. You can see that the column mean of $6.72 is for all of those who had the conventional program regardless of whether they have a high school diploma. The column mean of $8.78

A *main effect* results from examining one way in which participants were classified while ignoring the other.

is for all those who had the new program—some of whom had a high school diploma and some of whom did not have a diploma. Thus, by looking at the column means, only the effect of the type of program is being considered (and *not* the effect of a high school diploma). When researchers examine the effect of only one of the ways in which the participants were classified, they are examining a *main effect*.

> If there is a difference between the column means, this suggests one *main effect*.

Now, consider the row means of $8.82 (for those with a high school diploma) and $6.68 (for those without a high school diploma). This suggests that those with a diploma, on the average, have higher earnings than those without one. This is also a *main effect*. This main effect is for having a high school diploma while temporarily ignoring the type of training program. In other words, regardless of the type of program, those with a high school diploma earn more.

> If there is a difference between the row means, this suggests another *main effect*.

Up to this point, there are two findings that would be of interest to those studying welfare: (1) the new program seems to be superior to the conventional program in terms of hourly wages, and (2) those with a high school diploma seem to have higher hourly wages. (*Note*: The terms "seems to" and "seem to" are being used because only random samples have been studied. We do not yet know whether the differences are statistically significant in light of sampling error.)

You may already have noticed that there is a third interesting finding: Those with a high school diploma seem to earn about the same amount regardless of the program. This statement is based on these means for *those with a high school diploma* reproduced from the first row of the table in Example 1 on the previous page:

	Conventional program	New program
H.S. diploma	$M = \$8.88$	$M = \$8.75$

In contrast, those without a high school diploma seem to benefit more from the new program than the conventional one. This statement is based on these means for *those without a high school diploma* reproduced from the second row of the table in Example 1:

	Conventional program	New program
No H.S. diploma	$M = \$4.56$	$M = \$8.80$

Now, suppose you were the researcher who conducted this study. You are now an expert on the training programs for those on welfare, and an administrator calls you for advice. She asks you,

"Which program should we use? The conventional one or the new one?" You could, of course, tell her that there is a *main effect* for programs that suggests that, overall, the new program is superior in terms of wages. However, if this is all you told the administrator, your answer would be incomplete. A more complete answer would consist of two parts:

1. For those with a diploma, the two programs are about equal in effectiveness. Other things being equal, it is not important which program is used with welfare recipients who have a diploma.

2. For those without a diploma, however, the new program is superior to the conventional one. Other things being equal, those without a diploma should be assigned to the new program— not the conventional program.

Because you cannot give a complete answer about the two types of programs (which is only one of the two ways in which the participants were classified) without also referring to high school diplomas (the other way in which they were classified), we say there is an *interaction* between the two variables (i.e., an interaction between the type of program and whether participants have a diploma). In other words, how well the two programs work depends in part upon whether the participants have high school diplomas.

> When you cannot give a complete discussion about one *main effect* without discussing the other main effect, you have an *interaction*.

Here is a simple way in which you can spot an interaction when there are only two rows of means: Subtract each mean in the second row from the mean in the first row. If the two differences are the same, there is no interaction. If they are different, there is an interaction. Here is how it works for the data in Example 1 on page 133: ($8.88 − $4.56 = **$4.32** and $8.75 − $8.80 = **−$0.05**). Because **$4.32** is *not* the same as **−$0.05**, the data suggest that there is an interaction.

> You can spot an *interaction* by subtracting down the rows and comparing the differences.

	Type of program	
	Conventional	New
H.S. diploma	$M = \$8.88$	$M = \$8.75$
No H.S. diploma	$M = \$4.56$	$M = \$8.80$
Difference	**$4.32**	**−$0.05**

Consider Example 2 on the next page, in which there are no main effects but there is an interaction.

Example 2:

A random sample from a population of those suffering from a chronic illness was administered a new drug. Another random sample from the same population was administered a standard drug. Participants were also classified as to whether they were male or female. At the end of the study, improvement was measured on a scale from 0 (for no improvement) to 10 (for complete recovery). These means were obtained:

Example 2 has no *main effects* but has an *interaction*.

	Drug		
	Standard	New	**Row means**
Male	$M = 5.00$	$M = 7.00$	**$M = 6.00$**
Female	$M = 7.00$	$M = 5.00$	**$M = 6.00$**
Column means	**$M = 6.00$**	**$M = 6.00$**	

The two column means in Example 2 are the same. Thus, if we temporarily ignore whether participants are male or female, we would conclude that the two drugs are equally effective. To state it statistically, we would say that *there is no main effect for the drugs.*

The two row means are the same. Thus, if we temporarily ignore which drug was taken, we can conclude that males and females improved to the same extent. To state it statistically, we would say that *there is no main effect for gender.*

Of course, the interesting finding in Example 2 is the *interaction.* The standard drug works better for females and the new drug works better for males. Subtracting as we did to identify an interaction for Example 1, we obtain the differences for Example 2, which are shown below. Because –2.00 is not equal to 2.00, there is an interaction.

Sometimes, the *interaction* is the most interesting finding.

	Drug	
	Standard	New
Male	$M = 5.00$	$M = 7.00$
Female	$M = 7.00$	$M = 5.00$
Column means	**$M = -2.00$**	**$M = 2.00$**

Consider Example 3 on the next page, in which there are two main effects but no interaction.

Example 3:

Random samples of high and low achievers were assigned to one of two types of reinforcement during math lessons. Achievement on a math test at the end of the experiment was the outcome variable. The mean scores on the test were:

| | Type of reinforcement | | |
	Type A	Type B	**Row means**
High achievers	$M = 50.00$	$M = 30.00$	$M = 40.00$
Low achievers	$M = 40.00$	$M = 20.00$	$M = 30.00$
Column means	$M = 45.00$	$M = 25.00$	

Example 3 has two *main effects* but no *interaction.*

In Example 3 above, there seems to be a main effect for type of reinforcement as indicated by the difference between the column means (45.00 and 25.00). Thus, ignoring achievement levels temporarily, Type A seems to be more effective than Type B.

There also seems to be a main effect for achievement level as indicated by the difference between the row means (40.00 and 30.00). Thus, ignoring the type of reinforcement, high achievers score higher on the math test than low achievers.

There is no interaction, as indicated by the differences, which are shown below:

| | Type of reinforcement | |
	Type A	Type B
High achievers	$M = 50.00$	$M = 30.00$
Low achievers	$M = 40.00$	$M = 20.00$
Difference	$M = 10.00$	$M = 10.00$

What does this lack of an interaction indicate? It indicates that regardless of the type of reinforcement, high achievers are the same number of points higher than low achievers (i.e., 10 points). Put another way, regardless of whether students are high or low achievers, Type A reinforcement is better.[2]

In review, a two-way ANOVA examines two *main effects* and one *interaction*. Of course, because only random samples have been studied, null hypotheses should be tested. For each of the main effects and for the interaction, the null hypothesis states that there is no *true* difference—that the observed differences were created by random sampling errors. A two-way ANOVA will therefore test the two main

A two-way ANOVA will test the null hypotheses for the two *main effects* and the *interaction*.

effects and the interaction for significance. This is done by conducting three F tests (one for each of the three null hypotheses) and determining the probability associated with each. Typically, if a probability is .05 or less, the null hypothesis is rejected and the main effect or interaction being tested is declared to be statistically significant.

The results of a two-way ANOVA are usually organized in a table. While the entries in such tables sometimes vary,[3] the most important entries are shown in Example 4.

> Results of a two-way ANOVA are usually organized in a table.

Example 4:

Source	F	p
Achievement level	3.25	.042
Type of reinforcement	19.69	.001
Interaction (Ach. × Reinf.)	1.32	.210

The probabilities shown in Example 4 above indicate whether there is significance. Both main effects (i.e., achievement level and type of reinforcement) are statistically significant because the values of p are both less than .05, the most commonly used level for rejecting the null hypothesis. The interaction, however, is not significant because p is greater than .05, and the null hypothesis regarding this interaction should not be rejected. Thus, three null hypotheses have been tested with a single two-way ANOVA, and two of them have been rejected.

> The probabilities (p) indicate whether there is significance.

Endnotes

[1] Note that income in large populations is usually skewed, making the mean an inappropriate average (see Section 11); for these groups, assume that it was not skewed. Also note that the row means and column means were obtained by adding and dividing by two; this is appropriate only if the number of participants in all cells is equal. If it is not, compute the row and column means using the original raw scores.

[2] The basis for this second statement is that if you subtract across the rows, you get the same difference for each row. Earlier, you were told to subtract down columns; however, subtracting across the rows works equally well in determining whether there is an interaction.

[3] It is also common to include the degrees of freedom, the sums of squares, and mean squares in an ANOVA table. As mentioned in the previous section, these are of little interest to the typical consumer of research.

Exercise for Section 25

Factual Questions (Assume there are equal numbers of participants in each cell.)

Questions 1 through 3 refer to this information:

Two types of basketball instruction were used with random samples of participants who either had previous experience playing or did not have previous experience. The means indicate the proficiency at playing basketball at the end of treatment.

	Type of instruction		
	New	Conventional	**Row means**
Had previous experience	$M = 230.00$	$M = 200.00$	$M = 215.00$
Did not have previous experience	$M = 200.00$	$M = 230.00$	$M = 215.00$
Column means	$M = 215.00$	$M = 215.00$	

1. Does there seem to be a main effect for type of instruction?

2. Does there seem to be a main effect for experience?

3. Does there seem to be an interaction?

Questions 4 through 6 refer to this information:

Random samples of participants with back pain and with headache pain were randomly assigned to two types of pain relievers. The means below indicate the average amount of pain relief. A higher mean indicates greater pain relief.

	Type of pain		
	Back pain	Headache pain	**Row means**
Type A pain reliever	$M = 25.00$	$M = 20.00$	$M = 22.50$
Type B pain reliever	$M = 15.00$	$M = 10.00$	$M = 12.50$
Column means	$M = 20.00$	$M = 15.00$	

4. Does there seem to be a main effect for type of pain (back pain versus headache pain)?

5. Does there seem to be a main effect for type of pain reliever?

6. Does there seem to be an interaction?

Questions 7 through 9 refer to this ANOVA table:

Source	F	p
Age level (young, old)	13.25	.029
Region (north, south)	1.69	.321
Interaction (age × region)	15.32	.043

7. Is the main effect for age level statistically significant at the .05 level?

8. Can the null hypothesis for the main effect of region be rejected at the .05 level?

9. Is the interaction between age and region statistically significant at the .05 level?

Question for Discussion

10. Briefly describe a hypothetical study in which it would be appropriate to conduct a two-way ANOVA.

Section 26

Chi-Square

Frequently, research data are *nominal* (i.e., naming data, such as participants naming the political candidates for whom they plan to vote).[1] Because such data do not consist of scores, they do not directly permit the computation of means and standard deviations. Instead of reporting means and standard deviations for such data, researchers typically report the number of participants who named each category (e.g., named each political candidate) and the corresponding percentages. Example 1 illustrates such a report.

Example 1:

A random sample of 200 registered voters was drawn and asked which of two candidates for an elected office they planned to vote for. The data shown below indicate that a majority plans to vote for Candidate Smith.

Candidate Smith	*Candidate Doe*
$n = 110$ (55.0%)	$n = 90$ (45.0%)

Although the data in Example 1 suggest that Candidate Smith is preferred, keep in mind that only a random sample of 200 registered voters was surveyed. Therefore, it is possible, for instance, that the population of likely voters is evenly split, but that a difference of 10 percentage points (55% versus 45%) was obtained because of the sampling errors associated with random sampling. For this possibility, the *null hypothesis* states that there is no true difference in the population—that is, the population of registered voters is evenly split.

For Example 1, the *t* test and the *F* test (i.e., ANOVA) cannot be used to test the null hypothesis because they are tests of differences among means, but the results in the example do not consist of means. Instead, they consist of the numbers of cases (*n*) and percentages.

The appropriate test for the data under consideration in Example 1 is *chi-square*, whose symbol is χ^2. A chi-square test[2] is designed to test for differences among frequencies. As it turns out, a chi-square test for the data in Example 1 on the previous page indicates that the probability that the null hypothesis is a correct hypothesis is greater than 5 in 100 ($p > .05$). Thus, the null hypothesis cannot be rejected and the difference between the frequencies (110 versus 90) cannot be declared to be statistically significant.

Note that while chi-square compares frequencies, whatever it determines about the statistical significance of the frequencies is also true of the associated percentages. Thus, because the difference between the two frequencies is not statistically significant, the difference between the percentage is also not statistically significant.

Example 1 on the previous page contains data that call for a *one-way chi-square test* (also known as a *goodness of fit chi-square test*). This is because the participants are classified in only one way: according to the candidate for whom they plan to vote.

In contrast, Example 2 contains data that call for a *two-way chi-square test*. In this example, each participant is classified according to (1) whether he or she is a man or a woman and (2) the candidate for whom he or she plans to vote.

Example 2:

A random sample of 200 men and a random sample of 200 women were drawn and asked to name the candidate for whom they planned to vote. These data were obtained:

	Candidate Jones	Candidate Barnes
Men	$n = 80$	$n = 120$
Women	$n = 120$	$n = 80$

Inspection of the data in Example 2 suggests that Candidate Jones is a stronger candidate among women, while Candidate Barnes is a stronger candidate among men. If this pattern is true among all men and all women in the population, both candidates should take heed. For instance, Candidate Jones might consider ways to shore up her support among men without alienating the women while Candidate Barnes might do the opposite.

However, only a random sample was surveyed in Example 2. Thus, before acting on the results of the survey, the candidates should consider how likely it is that the observed differences in preferences between the two groups (men and women) were created by random sampling errors (i.e., the assertion made by the null hypothesis). As it

To test differences among frequencies, researchers use *chi-square*.

In a *one-way chi-square*, participants are classified in only one way.

In a *two-way chi-square*, participants are classified in two ways.

The data in Example 2 suggest a relationship between gender and preference for candidates.

turns out, for Example 2, the two-way chi-square test reveals that the probability that the null hypothesis is correct is less than 1 in 1,000 ($p < .001$). Thus, it is very unlikely that this pattern of differences is due to sampling errors. Thus, with a high degree of confidence, the candidates can rule out sampling error as an explanation for the pattern of differences between men and women.[3]

In Example 3, a sample from one population of participants was asked two questions, each of which provided nominal data.

Example 3:

A random sample of college students was asked (1) whether they think that IQ tests measure innate (i.e., inborn) intelligence and (2) whether they had taken a course in psychological testing. These data resulted:

	Took course	*Did not take course*
Yes, innate	$n = 20$	$n = 30$
No, not innate	$n = 40$	$n = 15$

The data in Example 3 above suggest that those who took the course are less likely to think that IQ tests measure innate intelligence (20 "yes" versus 40 "no") than those who did not take the course (30 "yes" versus 15 "no"). Thus, there appears to be a relationship between whether participants have taken the course and whether they believe IQ tests measure innate intelligence. However, only a random sample was questioned and, thus, it is possible that the observed relationship is only due to sampling error. That is, the null hypothesis asserts that there is no *true* relationship (in the population). As it turns out, a chi-square test for the data in Example 3 above produced this result:

$$\chi^2 = 11.455, df = 1, p < .001$$

Because $p < .001$, the null hypothesis can be rejected with a high degree of confidence. Note that the odds are less than 1 in 1,000 that the null hypothesis for the data in Example 3 above is a correct hypothesis.[4]

Example 4 on the next page shows how the results of the chi-square test for Example 3 above might be stated in a research report in an academic journal.

The data in Example 3 suggest a relationship between whether students have taken the course and what they believe IQ tests measure.

The chi-square test for Example 3 indicates that the null hypothesis should be rejected at the .001 level; the relationship is statistically significant.

Example 4:

The relationship was statistically significant with those who took a course in psychological testing being less likely to believe that IQ tests measure innate intelligence than those who have not taken the course ($\chi^2 = 11.455$, *df* = 1, *p* < .001).

Endnotes

[1] See Section 4 to review the meaning of the nominal scale of measurement.

[2] The tests on means (*t* and *F*) in earlier sections of this book are based on the assumption that the underlying distributions are normal; they are examples of *parametric tests*. Since chi-square is not based on such an assumption, it is an example of a *nonparametric* (or *distribution-free*) test.

[3] Example 2 illustrates that a two-way chi-square is used to test for a *relationship* between two variables. In this example, there is a significant relationship between the variable of gender and the variable of voters' preferences for candidates. In other words, how voters plan to vote is related to their gender.

[4] Notice that in the examples, the responses are independent. For instance, in Example 2, the gender of a person is not determined by his or her preference for a candidate. Also, each response category is mutually exclusive. For instance, a participant is not allowed to indicate that he/she is both male and female. Independent and mutually exclusive categories are assumptions underlying the chi-square test.

Exercise for Section 26

Factual Questions

1. If you calculated the mean math test score for freshmen and the mean math test score for seniors and wanted to compare the two means for statistical significance, would a chi-square test be appropriate? Explain.

2. If you asked members of a random sample which of two types of skin cream they prefer, and you wanted to compare the resulting frequencies with an inferential statistical test, would a chi-square test be appropriate?

3. If you asked members of a random sample (1) which of two types of skin cream they prefer and (2) whether they were satisfied with the condition of their skin, would a "one-way chi-square test" *or* a "two-way chi-square test" be appropriate?

4. If you asked members of a random sample whether they planned to vote "yes" or "no" on a ballot proposition, would a "one-way chi-square test" *or* a "two-way chi-square test" be appropriate?

5. For examining relationships for nominal data, should a researcher use a "one-way chi-square test" *or* a "two-way chi-square test"?

6. Suppose you read that "$\chi^2 = 4.111$, $df = 1$, $p < .05$." What decision should be made about the null hypothesis at the .05 level?

7. Suppose you read that "$\chi^2 = 7.418$, $df = 1$, $p < .01$." Is this statistically significant at the .01 level?

8. Suppose you read that "$\chi^2 = 2.824$, $df = 2$, $p > .05$." What decision should be made about the null hypothesis at the .05 level?

9. If as a result of a chi-square test, p is found to be less than .001, the odds that the null hypothesis is correct are less than 1 in _____?

Notes:

Section 27

Limitations of Significance Testing

You should recall the following four important concepts from your study of Sections 20 through 26:

Knowing the four basic concepts in significance testing will help you understand this section of this book.

1. The *null hypothesis* attributes differences to random sampling errors. In effect, it says that any differences observed in random samples (such as the difference between the means of an experimental and a control group) are only chance deviations from a true difference of zero in the population from which the samples were drawn.

2. When there is low probability that something is true, researchers reject it. Thus, if there is a low probability that the null hypothesis is true, such as $p < .05$, researchers reject the null hypothesis. (In Sections 22 through 26, you learned about some specific statistical tests that researchers use to determine the value of the probability for particular types of data.)

3. The lower the value of p, the more statistically significant the result, meaning that a researcher can be more confident that he or she is making the correct decision when rejecting a null hypothesis. For instance, if a researcher rejects a null hypothesis at p equal to .05, there are 5 chances in 100 that he or she is incorrectly rejecting it. In contrast, if a significance test allows a researcher to reject the null hypothesis at the .01 level, he or she is taking only 1 chance in 100 that the decision to reject it is incorrect.

4. When a null hypothesis has been rejected, a researcher declares the difference being tested to be *statistically significant*.

Typically, researchers hope to find that their differences are statistically significant (i.e., *reliable*, because it is unlikely that they are due only to random sampling). Furthermore, they hope that they will be highly significant at levels such as .01 or .001. This allows them to state in their research reports that the differences they have observed in their research *very probably* are highly reliable. Reliable results are ones that researchers can count on from observation to ob-

Researchers typically hope to identify statistically significant differences.

147

servation or study to study. Consider this analogy: If an employer says that an employee is "reliable," the employer means that the employee can be counted on—time after time—to perform his or her work in a consistent manner. Just as employers are seeking reliable employees, researchers are seeking to identify reliable differences.

Unfortunately, some individuals make the mistake of equating a significant (i.e., reliable) difference with a "large difference." As it turns out, just because a difference is reliable does not necessarily mean that it is a large difference. Consider Example 1, which illustrates that a small difference can be a reliable difference.

Example 1:

An individual notices that the number of minutes of daylight is very slightly larger on December 22 than on December 21 (the shortest day of the year). She decides to sample the next 75 years and make the same measurements. Year after year, she obtains the same small difference when comparing the number of minutes of daylight on December 21 with the number on December 22. Conducting a *t* test on the difference between the average number of minutes on December 21 and the average on December 22, she finds that she has identified a *statistically significant* (i.e., reliable) difference. Note, however, that while the difference is reliable, it is quite small.

In Section 22, you learned that there are three factors that are mathematically combined to determine the significance of the difference between two means. They are: (1) the size of the difference, (2) the size of the sample, and (3) the amount of variation from one observation to another. While the size of the difference in Example 1 above is small, the size of the sample is reasonably large ($n = 75$). More important, there is essentially no variation from year to year (e.g., the number of minutes of daylight on December 21 is the same for each of the 75 years). This lack of variation indicates that a highly reliable (i.e., statistically significant) difference has been observed (even though it is a small difference).

Example 1 above is an extreme example designed to help you grasp the concept that *even a small difference can be statistically significant.* It is important to note that small statistically significant differences are frequently reported in all the sciences, especially in the

> Just because a difference is statistically significant does not mean that it is a large difference.

> Even a small difference can be statistically significant.

148

social and behavioral sciences. Thus, for consumers of research, it is not sufficient to know that a difference is statistically significant; they also need to know the size of the difference. It is not uncommon for a researcher (or someone who is writing about another's research) to state that XYZ is statistically significantly higher than ABC—without discussing the magnitude of the difference—as though being statistically significant is equivalent to being large.

In practical terms, it is usually true that a small difference (even though it is significant) is less likely to be of practical importance than a large difference. However, it is also true that *even a small, significant difference can sometimes be important.* For instance, suppose that a researcher found that making only a very modest change in diet created a very small decrease in the side effects experienced by individuals who are undergoing chemotherapy. Suppose that the difference was statistically significant, indicating that it is a reliable difference. Is this small difference of practical importance? Arguably, those who are experiencing the side effects would probably find any degree of relief from side effects to be very important, especially because it involves only a very modest (and presumably inexpensive) change in diet.

> Even a small, significant difference can sometimes be important.

In light of the above discussion, you may be wondering why researchers conduct significance tests. The answer is clear if you keep in mind that the evaluation of a difference is a *three-step process* in which significance testing comes first. To make the discussion easy to follow, consider an experiment in which there is an experimental group and a control group, both of which were drawn at random. Assume that the difference between the mean of the experimental group is being compared with the mean of the control group with a *t* test for statistical significance. In order, the steps are:

> Evaluating a difference is a *three-step process* in which significance testing comes first.

1. First, use a significance test to determine if a difference is statistically significant (i.e., reliable and unlikely to be due to chance). If it is *not* statistically significant, proceed to Step 2. If it is statistically significant, skip Step 2 and proceed to Step 3 on the next page.

2. For an insignificant result, a researcher should *not* assert that the experimental treatment is superior to the control condition. At this point, a researcher might abandon the hypothesis underlying his or her research or decide to conduct a more rigorous experiment with a larger number of participants.

Note that if the treatment for the experimental group is one that is already in use (perhaps an unproven herbal treatment for depression that is already being advertised and sold in specialty stores), the result might have *practical implications*. In this example, for instance, the researcher might want to assert that, within the limitations of his or her study, a reliable effect was *not* found and that individuals probably do *not* benefit from consuming the herbal treatment. The practical implication would be that consumers probably should stop purchasing the herbal treatment. Thus, an insignificant difference might have a practical implication.

3. Evaluate a statistically significant difference in terms of its *practical significance*. In order to consider its practical significance, a researcher will need to consider the size of the difference[1] in relation to the benefit. In an experiment, the ideal is to find an inexpensive treatment (such as taking a small dosage of aspirin on a regular basis) that produces a large beneficial effect (such as a very large reduction of the incidence of heart attacks). However, if a treatment produces only a small (but statistically significant) difference, the cost of using the treatment becomes an important consideration. For instance, if an experiment revealed that a slight modification in the way teachers discuss the concept of simple fractions (an inexpensive treatment) produces, on average, a small increase in students' scores on a test on simple fractions, the treatment might be of practical value. (In other words, a very inexpensive treatment that produces a small, beneficial difference might be worth pursuing.) In contrast, if a small difference (such as a small difference in achievement test scores) comes at a very high price (such as having to purchase expensive computer-assisted instructional software for each student), the cost might mitigate the practical significance of the results.

Considering the second and third steps discussed above reveals that determining practical significance is a complex process that should be undertaken after conducting a significance test.

In conclusion, the fundamental limitations of significance testing are: (1) it fails to indicate the size of a difference, and (2) it does not assess the practical significance of a difference. Unfortunately, some researchers and reviewers who summarize and report on the research of others fail to recognize these limitations and assume that

---

An *insignificant* difference can have *practical implications*.

Consider the size of the difference when evaluating a statistically significant difference.

Consider the cost in relation to the benefit when evaluating a statistically significant difference.

Small significant differences might be worth pursuing if the cost is low. If the cost is high, they might be of limited practical significance.

There are two fundamental limitations of significance testing. Failure to recognize them can lead to misinterpretation of research results.

all statistically significant differences are inherently large and therefore of practical importance.[2] Their failure can lead them to misinterpret the results of research and make poor decisions that they claim to be "research-based."

Endnotes

[1] See Appendix E near the end of this book for a discussion of how statisticians standardize the quantification of the size of the differences between pairs of means.

[2] As you know from Section 19, it is true that the larger the difference between two means, the more likely it is statistically significant. However, as you also know, the sample size and the amount of variation also contribute to the decision regarding statistical significance. Failure to recognize that *three* factors contribute to the decision regarding statistical significance (not just the size of the difference) probably contributes to some of the confusion and misinterpretation of the results of significance testing.

Exercise for Section 27

Factual Questions

1. To what does the null hypothesis attribute differences?

2. When should the null hypothesis be rejected? (Circle one.)
   A. When the probability is low.   B. When the probability is high.

3. Is the statement that "the difference is statistically significant" completely equivalent to saying "the difference is large"?

4. Can a small difference be statistically significant?

5. Can a small, significant difference sometimes be important?

6. Is it possible for an insignificant difference to have practical implications?

7. In an experiment, what is the "ideal" finding regarding cost in relation to benefit?

8. Should practical significance be determined before determining statistical significance?

9. According to this section, is determining practical significance a complex process?

Question for Discussion

10. Suppose a student made this statement: "Research shows that treatment with Alpha is significantly better than the Beta Treatment." How would you respond to this student? Would you ask for additional information based on what you learned from this section? Explain.

Appendix A

Computation of the Standard Deviation

To compute the standard deviation for a large number of scores, a computer should be used. However, considering how the standard deviation is computed using a formula can help in understanding its meaning.

The formula that defines the standard deviation is:

$$S = \sqrt{\frac{\Sigma x^2}{N}}$$

The lowercase x stands for the deviation of a score from the mean of its distribution. To obtain it, first calculate the mean (in this case, $78/6 = 13.00$) and subtract the mean from each score, as shown in Example 1. Then square the deviations and sum the squares, as indicated by the symbol Σ. Then enter this value in the formula along with the number of cases (N) and perform the calculations as indicated below.

Example 1:

Scores (X)	Deviations ($X - M$)	Squared Deviations (x^2)
10	$10 - 13.00 = -3$	9.00
11	$11 - 13.00 = -2$	4.00
11	$11 - 13.00 = -2$	4.00
13	$13 - 13.00 = 0$	0.00
14	$14 - 13.00 = 1$	1.00
19	$19 - 13.00 = 6$	36.00
		$\Sigma x^2 = 54.00$

Thus, substituting the sum of the squared deviations (54) and the number of cases (6 scores) in the formula:

$$S = \sqrt{\frac{54}{6}} = \sqrt{9.00} = 3.00$$

As the formula indicates, the standard deviation is the *square root of the average squared deviation from the mean*. Thus, the larger the deviations from the mean, the larger the standard deviation. Conversely, the smaller the deviations from the mean, the smaller the standard deviation. At the extreme, when all the scores are the same, the standard deviation equals zero, as indicated in Example 2, where each score is 20 and therefore the mean of the scores is also 20 (i.e., 20.00).

Example 2:

Scores (X)	Deviations ($X - M$)	Squared Deviations (x^2)
20	$20 - 20.00 = 0$	0.00
20	$20 - 20.00 = 0$	0.00
20	$20 - 20.00 = 0$	0.00
20	$20 - 20.00 = 0$	0.00
20	$20 - 20.00 = 0$	0.00
20	$20 - 20.00 = 0$	0.00
		$\Sigma x^2 = 0.00$

Thus, substituting the sum of the squared deviations (0.00) and the number of cases (6 scores) in the formula:

$$S = \sqrt{\frac{0.00}{6}} = \sqrt{0.00} = 0.00$$

Thus, when there is no variation (i.e., all scores are the same), the standard deviation equals 0.00.

Appendix B

Notes on Interpreting Pearson *r* and Linear Regression

This appendix describes why a Pearson *r* may be misleadingly low and introduces a statistical procedure for making predictions for individuals when there is a reasonably strong relationship as indicated by a Pearson *r*.

Why the Pearson r May Be Misleadingly Low

The value of a Pearson *r* can be misleadingly low for two reasons. First, its value is diminished if the variability in a group is artificially low. For the sake of illustration, assume that we wanted to study the relationship between height and weight in the adult population but foolishly selected only participants who were all exactly six feet tall. When weighing them, we would undoubtedly find some variation in their weights. What is the correlation between height and weight among such a group? Even though there is a positive relationship between the two variables in the general adult population, the correlation in this odd sample is zero. This must be the result because those who weigh more and those who weigh less are all of the same height. (This sample cannot show that those who are taller tend to weigh more because all subjects are of the same height. Thus, the value of the Pearson *r* will equal 0.00.)

A more realistic example is the relationship between scores on a college admissions test and grades earned in college. Although the test is given to all applicants in order to make admissions decisions about all of them, grades are available only for those who were admitted, and the correlation between scores and grades can be computed only for those applicants on whom we have complete data. Unfortunately, those for whom we have complete data are those who tend to have higher scores. Thus, the scores of those who are admitted are less variable than the scores of all applicants (since the low-scoring applicants were not admitted). As a result, the value of the Pearson *r* will be lower than would be obtained if we correlated using scores and grades for *all* applicants.

The second reason that an *r* can be misleadingly low is if *r* is computed for a curvilinear relationship. For instance, the relationship between test-taking anxiety and performance on standardized tests might be curvilinear. That is, small amounts of anxiety might be beneficial in motivating examinees to do well on a test, but larger amounts of anxiety might be detrimental. Thus, as anxiety increases, up to a point there is a positive relationship with anxiety; after reaching a critical point, as anxiety increases there is a negative relationship. If the Pearson *r* is computed for such data, the negative part of the relationship will cancel out the positive part, yielding an *r* near zero. Pearson recognized this problem and warned against using his statistic for describing curvilinear relationships. Other techniques such as the *correlation ratio,* which are beyond the scope of this book, are available for describing curvilinear relationships. Fortunately, such relationships are relatively rare in the social and behavioral sciences.

Making Specific Predictions for Individuals

Suppose you found a reasonably high value of the Pearson *r*, such as *r* = .60, between scores on a college admissions test and grades earned in a college.[1] This indicates that the admissions test is a reasonably valid predictor of grades. It does not indicate, however, how to make specific predictions for individuals who might apply to the college in the future. For example, if Marilyn has an admissions test score of 600, the Pearson *r* of .60 does not tell us what specific grade point average to predict that Marilyn will earn. *Linear regression* is a statistical technique that enables us to make such predictions under most circumstances. It is beyond the scope of this book to describe this procedure, but students who have mastered correlational concepts may wish to pursue it in other books, including *Success at Statistics*, which is available from Pyrczak Publishing.

---

[1] In practice, values of the Pearson *r* for relationships between admissions test scores and grades earned in college rarely exceed .60 and often are substantially lower.

Appendix C

Table of Random Numbers

Row #																		
1	2	1	0	4	9	8	0	8	8	8	0	6	9	2	4	8	2	6
2	0	7	3	0	2	9	4	8	2	7	8	9	8	9	2	9	7	1
3	4	4	9	0	0	2	8	6	2	6	7	7	3	1	2	5	1	
4	7	3	2	1	1	2	0	7	7	6	0	3	8	3	4	7	8	1
5	3	3	2	5	8	3	1	7	0	1	4	0	7	8	9	3	7	7
6	6	1	2	0	5	7	2	4	4	0	0	6	3	0	2	8	0	7
7	7	0	9	3	3	3	7	4	0	4	8	8	9	3	5	8	0	5
8	7	5	1	9	0	9	1	5	2	6	5	0	9	0	3	5	8	8
9	3	5	6	9	6	5	0	1	9	4	6	6	7	5	6	8	3	1
10	8	5	0	3	9	4	3	4	0	6	5	1	7	4	4	6	2	7
11	0	5	9	6	8	7	4	8	1	5	5	0	5	1	7	1	5	8
12	7	6	2	2	6	9	6	1	9	7	1	1	4	7	1	6	2	0
13	3	8	4	7	8	9	8	2	2	1	6	3	8	7	0	4	6	1
14	1	9	1	8	4	5	6	1	8	1	2	4	4	4	2	7	3	4
15	1	5	3	6	7	6	1	8	4	3	1	8	8	7	7	6	0	4
16	0	5	5	3	6	0	7	1	3	8	1	4	6	7	0	4	3	5
17	2	2	3	8	6	0	9	1	9	0	4	4	7	6	8	1	5	1
18	2	3	3	2	5	5	7	6	9	4	9	7	1	3	7	9	3	8
19	8	5	5	0	5	3	7	8	5	4	5	1	6	0	4	8	9	1
20	0	6	1	1	3	4	8	6	4	3	2	9	4	3	8	7	4	1
21	9	1	1	8	2	9	0	6	9	6	9	4	2	9	9	0	6	0
22	3	7	8	0	6	3	7	1	2	6	5	2	7	6	5	6	5	1
23	5	3	0	5	1	2	1	0	9	1	3	7	5	6	1	2	5	0
24	7	2	4	8	6	7	9	3	8	7	6	0	9	1	6	5	7	8
25	0	9	1	6	7	0	3	8	0	9	1	5	4	2	3	2	4	5
26	3	8	1	4	3	7	9	2	4	5	1	2	8	7	7	4	1	3

Notes:

Appendix D

More About the Null Hypothesis

Suppose you have a *directional research hypothesis* (H_1) that states that the population mean for Group 1 (μ_1) is higher than the population mean for Group 2 (μ_2). In other words, if the population mean for Group 2 is subtracted from the population mean for Group 1, the difference is greater than zero. Using symbols, this is how it is stated:

H_1: $\mu_1 - \mu_2 > 0$

The *null hypothesis* (H_0) that complements the research hypothesis states that if the population mean for Group 2 is subtracted from the population mean for Group 1, the difference is either zero or less than zero. Using symbols, this is how it is stated:

H_0: $\mu_1 - \mu_2 \leq 0$

For reasons beyond the scope of this book, significance tests of this null hypothesis are more liberal than tests of the null hypothesis described in Part D of this book. That is, tests of this null hypothesis are more likely to lead to rejection of the null hypothesis. Such tests are called *one-tailed tests*.

Notes:

Appendix E

Effect Size for the Difference Between Two Means

Suppose a researcher uses a test or scale with which you are very familiar. When he or she reports that the difference between the experimental and control groups is such-and-such a number of points, you will have a good idea of how large and important the difference is. However, very often you will not be familiar with the tests and instruments used in research. This makes it difficult for you to assess whether the difference is "large."

In recent years, it has become increasingly popular to *standardize* differences between means with a statistic that describes *effect size*. One of the most widely used ones is a statistic known as Cohen's *d*. This statistic is quite easy to compute. Simply subtract the control group mean from the experimental group mean and divide by the standard deviation of the control group.[1] The following is an example. Suppose Researcher A used a scale with possible score values from 0 to 100 and obtained these results:

Experimental Group: $M = 40.00$, $SD = 11.00$

Control Group: $M = 30.00$, $SD = 10.00$

Cohen's $d = (40.00 - 30.00)/10 = 1.00$

If we read a report that states that *d* equals 1.00 (based on the statistics shown immediately above), what does this indicate? Simply this: The mean of the experimental group is a full standard deviation higher than the mean of the control group. Is this large? Yes, it is quite large. Remember that there are only about three standard deviation units above (and below) the mean and that the vast majority of cases are within one standard deviation of the mean. Hence, if the average (mean) participant in the experimental group is a full standard deviation above the average participant in the control group (i.e., *d* = 1.00), the average experimental group person is higher than the vast majority of those in the control group.

The term *standardize* was used above. As it turns out, using *d* standardizes our descriptions of the sizes of differences. To illustrate this, consider Researcher B, who studied the same phenomena but used a scale with scores that could range from 200 to 800 and obtained these statistics:

---

[1] Some statisticians calculate a special type of average of the standard deviations for the control and experimental groups called the pooled standard deviation, and use it as the divisor.

Experimental Group: $M = 400.00$, $SD = 110.00$

Control Group: $M = 300.00$, $SD = 100.00$

Cohen's $d = (400.00 - 300.00)/100 = 1.00$

Notice that d is the same in both examples even though very different scales were used. Researcher A got a 10-point raw difference while Researcher B got a 100-point raw difference. However, by dividing the corresponding control group's standard deviation into each of these differences, we find that the *effect size* (size of the difference) is the same ($d = 1.00$) in both cases. This standardization takes place because d expresses each difference in terms of standard deviation units, which usually range from three below to three above the mean. Put another way, using *standard* deviation units as a way of looking at differences *standardizes* the process.

There are no universally accepted guidelines for attaching labels to values of d. However, it is safe to say that most statisticians would refer to values of about 0.30 as indicating a moderately large difference, 0.50 as indicating a large difference, and 0.75 and above as indicating a very large difference.

It is important to keep in mind that while using values of d is a meaningful and convenient way to standardize discussions and comparisons of differences, it does not establish the *practical significance* of differences. For instance, the very large differences we considered above (with $d = 1.00$ in each case) might not be of practical significance if the costs of producing the differences are too great for widespread use. (See Section 27 for additional information on practical versus statistical significance.)

Comprehensive Review Questions

Section 1: The Empirical Approach to Knowledge

1. The *empirical* approach to knowledge is based on
   A. deduction.
   B. reliance on authority.
   C. observation.

2. "Everyday observation is an example of the empirical approach to knowledge." This statement is
   A. true.   B. false.

3. If there are 800 teachers in a school district and 100 are selected for observation, the 100 are known as a
   A. population.
   B. sample.

4. "Flawed research can be as misleading as everyday observations." This statement is
   A. true.   B. false.

5. What is a primary function of statistical analysis?
   A. Planning when observations will be made.
   B. Organizing and summarizing data.
   C. Identifying a population.

Section 2: Types of Empirical Research

1. Treatments are given in which type of study?
   A. Experimental.
   B. Nonexperimental.

2. Treatments constitute which type of variable?
   A. Independent.
   B. Dependent.

3. Suppose students were treated with two types of rewards to see which one was more effective in promoting spelling achievement. *Spelling achievement* is the
   A. independent variable.
   B. dependent variable.

4. Researchers try to change the participants in which type of study?
   A. Experimental.
   B. Descriptive.

5. A survey is an example of
   A. an experimental study.
   B. a nonexperimental study.

Section 3: Introduction to Sampling

1. *Parameters* are based on a study of a
   A. sample.
   B. population.

2. "Using volunteers when sampling is presumed to create a bias." This statement is
   A. true.   B. false.

3. What is the most important characteristic of a good sample?
   A. Being free from bias.
   B. Being large.

4. "Random sampling creates sampling errors." This statement is
   A. true.   B. false.

5. Using random sampling identifies
   A. an accidental sample.
   B. a sample of convenience.
   C. an unbiased sample.

Section 4: Scales of Measurement

1. If participants name their county of residence, the resulting data are at what level?
   A. Ordinal.
   B. Interval.
   C. Ratio.
   D. Nominal.

2. If a teacher ranks students from low to high on their volleyball skills, he or she is measuring at what level?
   A. Ordinal.
   B. Interval.
   C. Ratio.
   D. Nominal.

3. Which two scales of measurement tell us by *how much* participants differ from each other?
   A. Ordinal and nominal.
   B. Interval and ordinal.
   C. Ratio and interval.
   D. Nominal and interval.

4. "The ordinal scale is a higher level of measurement than the interval scale." This statement is
   A. true.   B. false.

5. "Measuring height using a tape measure is an example of the ratio scale of measurement." This statement is
   A. true.   B. false.

Section 5: Descriptive, Correlational, and Inferential Statistics

1. Which of the following is used to summarize data?
   A. Inferential statistics.
   B. Descriptive statistics.

2. If there is a perfect correlation, what is the value of the correlation coefficient?
   A. 0.00.
   B. 1.00.
   C. Some other value.

3. "It is necessary to use inferential statistics when conducting a census." This statement is
   A. true.   B. false.

4. "All populations are large." This statement is
   A. true.   B. false.

5. Which type of statistics tells researchers how much confidence they can have when they generalize from samples to populations?
   A. Inferential.
   B. Descriptive.

Section 6: Frequencies, Percentages, and Proportions

1. "In descriptive statistics, the lowercase letter f stands for *function*." This statement is
   A. true.   B. false.

2. If there are 1,000 citizens in a town and 53% favor capital punishment, how many favor it?
   A. 53.
   B. 530.
   C. Some other number.

3. If 30 out of 100 parents favor school uniforms, what percentage favors them?
   A. 30%.
   B. 60%.
   C. 90%.
   D. Some other percentage.

4. "For a proportion of .22, the corresponding percentage is 2.2%." This statement is
   A. true.   B. false.

5. "When reporting percentages, it is desirable to also report the underlying frequencies." This statement is
   A. true.   B. false.

Section 7: Shapes of Distributions

1. "A frequency polygon is a drawing that shows how many participants have each score." This statement is
   A. true.   B. false.

2. "A normal curve is also called a skewed curve." This statement is
   A. true.   B. false.

3. When a curve has a tail to the left but no tail to the right, it is said to have a
   A. positive skew.
   B. negative skew.

4. "Income in large populations is usually skewed to the right." This statement is
   A. true.   B. false.

5. "Another name for a skewed curve is 'bell-shaped curve.'" This statement is
   A. true.   B. false.

Section 8: The Mean: An Average

1. "The uppercase letter X without a bar over it is a symbol for the mean." This statement is
   A. true.   B. false.

2. "The mean is the most frequently used average." This statement is
   A. true.   B. false.

3. "In a set of scores, the deviations from the mean have a sum of zero." This statement is
   A. true.   B. false.

4. The mean is associated with which scales of measurement?
   A. Ordinal and nominal.
   B. Interval and ordinal.
   C. Nominal and interval.
   D. Ratio and interval.

5. "The mean is an especially good average for describing skewed distributions." This statement is
   A. true.   B. false.

Section 9: Mean, Median, and Mode

1. Which average is defined as the *most frequently occurring score*?
   A. Mean.
   B. Median.
   C. Mode.

2. If the median for a set of scores equals 75, what percentage of the scores is below 75?
   A. 25%.
   B. 50%.
   C. 100%.
   D. Some other percentage.

3. "The mean is insensitive to extreme scores." This statement is
   A. true.   B. false.

4. "In a distribution with a negative skew, the median has a higher value than the mean." This statement is
A. true. B. false.

5. What is the mode of the following scores?
Scores: 1, 2, 3, 6, 6, 6
A. 3.
B. 4.
C. 6.
D. Some other value.

Section 10: Range and Interquartile Range

1. "A synonym for the term *variability* is *dispersion*." This statement is
A. true. B. false.

2. "The *range* is a statistic that describes central tendency." This statement is
A. true. B. false.

3. Scores that lie far outside the range of the vast majority of scores are known as
A. *IQR*s.
B. outliers.
C. median points.

4. "The interquartile range is defined as the range of the middle 50% of the participants." This statement is
A. true. B. false.

5. "The interquartile range is unduly affected by outliers." This statement is
A. true. B. false.

Section 11: Standard Deviation

1. "The standard deviation is a frequently used measure of variability." This statement is
A. true. B. false.

2. Which group has a larger standard deviation?
A. Scores for Group I: 0, 5, 10, 15, 20.
B. Scores for Group II: 1, 2, 3, 4, 5.

3. "If all participants have the same score, the value of the standard deviation is 1.00." This statement is
A. true. B. false.

4. In a normal distribution, what percentage of the cases lies between the mean and one standard deviation unit above the mean?
A. 34%
B. 50%
C. 68%

5. In a normal distribution with a mean of 50.00 and a standard deviation of 8.00, what percentage of the cases lies between scores of 42 and 58?
A. 34%
B. 50%
C. 68%

Section 12: Correlation

1. For the scores on Test X and Test Y shown below, there is
A. a direct relationship.
B. an inverse relationship.
C. no relationship.

Student	Test X	Test Y
Janice	25	9
Brittany	30	7
Ramon	35	4
Wallace	40	1

2. For the scores on Test D and Test E shown below, there is
A. a direct relationship.
B. an inverse relationship.
C. no relationship.

Student	Test D	Test E
Buddy	303	20
Turner	343	53
Kathy	479	70
Suzanne	599	88

3. "A *direct* relationship is sometimes called a *positive* relationship." This statement is
A. true. B. false.

4. "In an inverse relationship, those who are high on one variable tend to be low on the other." This statement is
A. true. B. false.

5. "*Correlation* is the best way to examine cause-and-effect." This statement is
A. true. B. false.

Section 13: Pearson *r*

1. When there is a perfect, inverse relationship, what is the value of *r*?
A. 1.00.
B. 0.00.
C. –1.00.
D. Some other value.

2. "It is possible for a relationship to be both inverse and strong." This statement is
A. true. B. false.

3. Which of the following values of *r* represents the strongest relationship?
   A. .64.
   B. −.79.
   C. 0.00.

4. "An *r* of .60 is equivalent to 60%." This statement is
   A. true.   B. false.

5. "An *r* of −.95 represents a stronger relationship than an *r* of .88." This statement is
   A. true.   B. false.

Section 14: Coefficient of Determination

1. "The symbol for the coefficient of determination is r^2." This statement is
   A. true.   B. false.

2. If the Pearson *r* equals .30, the coefficient of determination is calculated by
   A. taking the square root of .30.
   B. multiplying .30 by .30.

3. "For an *r* of .80, the ability to predict is 64% better than zero." This statement is
   A. true.   B. false.

4. When a coefficient of determination equals .20, what percentage of the variance on one variable is *not* predicted by the other variable?
   A. 4%
   B. 20%
   C. 96%
   D. Some other percentage.

5. "When *r* = .40, the percentage of variance accounted for is 16%." This statement is
   A. true.   B. false.

Section 15: Scattergram

1. Scattergrams are presented in research reports
   A. frequently.
   B. infrequently.

2. The more scatter in a scattergram, the
   A. stronger the relationship.
   B. weaker the relationship.

3. "In the social and behavioral sciences, it is common to find scattergrams in which all the dots are on a single, straight line." This statement is
   A. true.
   B. false.

4. "When the dots in a scattergram form a pattern from the lower left to the upper right, the relationship is inverse." This statement is
   A. true.
   B. false.

5. "Each dot in a scattergram stands for the two scores of one participant." This statement is
   A. true.
   B. false.

Section 16: Multiple Correlation

1. When low scores on one variable are associated with low scores on the other variable, this suggests that the relationship is
   A. direct.   B. inverse.

2. Which of the following values of *R* represents the weakest relationship?
   A. $R^2 = 1.00$.
   B. $R^2 = -.96$.
   C. $R^2 = .22$.

3. For determining the correlation between one variable as a predictor of a second variable, which of the following should be computed?
   A. *R*.   B. *r*.

4. If $R^2 = .75$, what percentage of the variance is accounted for?
   A. 25%.   B. 75%.

5. Suppose a researcher is examining the validity of a combination of scores on a spatial relations test and previous math grades as a predictor of geometry grades. Which correlational statistic should the researcher compute for this research problem?
   A. *R*.   B. *r*.

Section 17: Variations on Random Sampling

1. Putting the names of girls in one hat and those of boys in another hat, and drawing out 20% of the girls' names and 20% of the boys' names separately from each hat constitutes
   A. cluster sampling.
   B. stratified random sampling.
   C. simple random sampling.

2. Which of the following usually creates less sampling error?
   A. Simple random sampling.
   B. Stratified random sampling.

3. "Using stratified random sampling eliminates all sampling errors." This statement is
   A. true.   B. false.

4. Suppose there are 500 people in a population and you want to draw a sample using a table of random numbers. Which of the following would be an appropriate number name for the first person to whom you assign a number before using the table?
   A. 00.
   B. 01.
   C. 05.
   D. 001.

5. Suppose a researcher randomly selected 10 classrooms (as clusters). Each classroom had 20 students. The researcher should report the sample size as
   A. 10.　B. 20.　C. 200.

Section 18: Sample Size

1. Increasing sample size
   A. increases precision.
   B. decreases bias.
   C. increases precision *and* decreases bias.

2. Which of the following will produce a greater reduction in sampling errors?
   A. Increasing the size of a sample from 800 to 900 (an increase of 100).
   B. Increasing the size of a sample from 200 to 300 (an increase of 100).

3. "The smaller the anticipated difference between groups, the larger the sample size should be." This statement is
   A. true.　B. false.

4. "For samples with very limited variability, even small samples can yield precise results." This statement is
   A. true.　B. false.

5. "It is usually better to use a small, unbiased sample than a large, biased one." This statement is
   A. true.　B. false.

Section 19: Standard Error of the Mean

1. "Using random sampling guarantees freedom from sampling errors." This statement is
   A. true.　B. false.

2. "According to the central limit theorem, the sampling distribution of means is skewed." This statement is
   A. true.　B. false.

3. The larger the variability in a population, the
   A. larger the standard error of the mean.
   B. smaller the standard error of the mean.

4. If $m = 40.00$ and $SE_M = 3.00$, what are the limits of the 68% confidence interval for the mean?
   A. 37.00 and 40.00.
   B. 40.00 and 43.00.
   C. 37.00 and 43.00.
   D. Some other values.

5. If you increase the sample size, what effect does this have on the size of the standard error of the mean?
   A. It increases it.
   B. It decreases it.

Section 20: Introduction to the Null Hypothesis

1. Which of the following is a correct statement of the null hypothesis?
   A. There is a true difference between the means.
   B. There is no true difference between the means.

2. Which of the following is a symbol for the null hypothesis?
   A. H_0.
   B. H_1.

3. "For a given study, the research hypothesis and the null hypothesis usually say the same thing." This statement is
   A. true.　B. false.

4. Which type of hypothesis predicts that one particular group's mean will be higher than another group's mean?
   A. Directional hypothesis.
   B. Nondirectional hypothesis.
   C. Null hypothesis.

5. The null hypothesis states that the true difference between the means
   A. equals zero.
   B. is greater than zero.
   C. is less than zero.

Section 21: Decisions About the Null Hypothesis

1. Which of the following yields a probability?
   A. A descriptive statistic.
   B. A significance test.

2. At what point is it conventional to reject the null hypothesis?
   A. When the probability is less than .05.
   B. When the probability is greater than .05.

3. The null hypothesis can be rejected with the greatest confidence when which one of the following is true?
   A. $p < .05$.
   B. $p < .01$.
   C. $p < .001$.

4. Rejecting the null hypothesis when in reality it is true is known as a
   A. Type I Error.
   B. Type II Error.

5. By conventional standards, if $p < .01$, researchers declare the difference to be statistically
   A. insignificant.
   B. significant.

Section 22: Introduction to the *t* Test

1. "A *t* test yields a probability." This statement is
   A. true. B. false.

2. "The smaller the sample, the more likely the null hypothesis will be rejected." This statement is
   A. true. B. false.

3. Under which of the following circumstances is the null hypothesis more likely to be rejected?
   A. When there is a small observed difference between means.
   B. When there is a large observed difference between means.

4. "Dependent data may have less sampling error than independent data." This statement is
   A. true. B. false.

5. If participants are matched (i.e., paired) across experimental and control groups, the resulting data are
   A. independent.
   B. dependent.

Section 23: Reports of the Results of *t* Tests

1. "Reporting a *t* test makes it unnecessary to report the values of the means and standard deviations." This statement is
   A. true. B. false.

2. If you read that $t = 0.452$, $df = 100$, $p > .05$, what should you conclude?
   A. The difference is statistically significant.
   B. The difference is not statistically significant.

3. "If a *t* test yields $p < .05$, the null hypothesis normally would be rejected." This statement is
   A. true. B. false.

4. If a researcher rejects the null hypothesis, what else is true?
   A. The difference is statistically significant.
   B. The difference is not statistically significant.

5. "It is safe to assume that if a difference is statistically significant, it is of practical significance." This statement is
   A. true. B. false.

Section 24: One-Way ANOVA

1. "ANOVA can be used to test for the difference(s) between only two means." This statement is
   A. true. B. false.

2. "The acronym *ANOVA* stands for *Analysis of Variance*." This statement is
   A. true. B. false.

3. For the typical consumer of research, which one of the following values in an ANOVA table is of greatest interest?
   A. Mean squares.
   B. The value of *p*.
   C. The value of *F*.

4. Suppose you read the following: $F = 0.641$, $df = 3$, 29, $p > .05$. What conclusion would you normally draw about the null hypothesis?
   A. Reject it.
   B. Do not reject it.

5. Suppose you read the following: $F = 3.50$, $df = 2$, 20, $p < .05$. What conclusion would you normally draw about statistical significance?
   A. It is statistically significant.
   B. It is not statistically significant.

Section 25: Two-Way ANOVA

1. Suppose participants were classified according to their religion and their country of origin in order to compare means for both religious groups and national origin groups. This would call for a
   A. one-way ANOVA.
   B. two-way ANOVA.

2. In order to examine an *interaction*, you
   A. temporarily ignore one way that the participants were classified while examining the results of the other way they were classified.
   B. look at both ways participants were classified at the same time in order to see how the two classification variables affect each other.

3. "In the table below, there appears to be an interaction." This statement is
   A. true.   B. false.

	X	Y
D	M = 40.00	M = 30.00
E	M = 30.00	M = 40.00

4. "In the table below, there appears to be an interaction." This statement is
   A. true.   B. false.

	S	T
U	M = 300.00	M = 200.00
V	M = 350.00	M = 250.00

5. "In the table below, there appears to be two main effects." This statement is
   A. true.   B. false.

	I	J
G	M = 40.00	M = 50.00
H	M = 30.00	M = 20.00

Section 26: Chi-Square

1. "For nominal data, researchers normally report frequencies and percentages instead of means and standard deviations." This statement is
   A. true.   B. false.

2. The symbol for chi-square is
   A. p
   B. r^2
   C. χ^2
   D. p^2

3. "For the data in the following table, a two-way chi-square would be an appropriate test of significance." This statement is
   A. true.   B. false.

	Happy	Unhappy
Boys	n = 30	n = 40
Girls	n = 40	n = 30

4. Suppose you read that as the result of a chi-square test, $p < .001$. By conventional standards, what decision should be made about the null hypothesis?
   A. Reject it.
   B. Do not reject it.

5. Suppose you read that as the result of a chi-square test, $p < .05$. By conventional standards, what decision should be made about statistical significance?
   A. It is significant.
   B. It is not significant.

Section 27: Limitations of Significance Testing

1. "For the difference between two means, the null hypothesis says that the difference is large." This statement is
   A. true.   B. false.

2. "Equating a significant difference with a large difference is a mistake." This statement is
   A. true.   B. false.

3. Is the size of the sample one of the factors that contributes to determining statistical significance?
   A. Yes.   B. No.

4. Can a very small difference between two means be statistically significant?
   A. Yes.   B. No.

5. Evaluating a difference is a three-step process. What is the first step?
   A. Determining if it is statistically significant.
   B. Considering the practical implications of an insignificant difference.
   C. Considering the practical implications of a statistically significant difference.

Notes: